980.3   Harner
JIVARO   The Jivaro

O

D096860

B77

980.3   Harner, Michael J
JIVARO   The Jivaro; people of the sacred water-
           falls [by] Michael J. Harner.   Garden City,
           N. Y., Published for the American Museum of
           Natural History [by] Doubleday/Natural His-
           tory Press, 1972.
              233 p. illus. 22cm

              Includes bibliograph

           1. Jivaro Indians.
           F3722.1.J5   H37

3 1232 00113 7886

Jívaro killer or *kakaram* ("powerful one") wearing bird bone shoulder ornament which symbolizes his possession of *arutam* soul power (Río Cusuimi, 1956–57).

THE JÌVARO

People of the Sacred Waterfalls

MICHAEL J. HARNER

Published for the American Museum of Natural History

Doubleday/Natural History Press

Garden City, New York

1972

Portions of the chapter, "The Hidden World," first
appeared, in slightly different form, as "Jívaro Souls,"
in *American Anthropologist*, Volume 64, Number 2,
1962, and as "The Sound of Rushing Water," in
Natural History magazine, June/July 1968. Permission to use this material is hereby gratefully acknowledged.

ISBN: 0-385-07118-3
Library of Congress Catalog Card Number 70-132496

To the Jívaro,

the

untsuri šuarä.

Amiči, puhuutarum!

CONTENTS

MAPS

FIGURES

INTRODUCTION

Only one tribe of American Indians is known ever to have successfully revolted against the empire of Spain and to have thwarted all subsequent attempts by the Spaniards to re-conquer them: the Jívaro (hee'-va-ro), the *untsuri šuarä* of eastern Ecuador. From 1599 onward they remained uncon-quered in their forest fastness east of the Andes, despite the fact that they were known to occupy one of the richest placer gold deposit regions in all of South America.

Tales of their fierceness became part of the folklore of Latin America, and their warlike reputation spread in the late nineteenth and early twentieth centuries when Jívaro "shrunken head" trophies, *tsantsa*, found their way to the mar-kets of exotica in the Western world. As occasional travelers visited them in the first decades of this century, the Jívaro also became known not as just a warlike group, but as an individ-ualistic people intensely jealous of their freedom and un-willing to be subservient to authority, even among them-selves. It was this quality that particularly attracted me when I went to study their way of life in 1956–57 and I was most fortunate, at that time, to find, especially east of the Cordil-lera de Cutucú, a portion of the Jívaro still unconquered and still living, with some changes, their traditional life style. This book is about their culture.

A factor that contributed to my decision to do fieldwork among the Jívaro was the incredible volume of contradictory and often obviously unreliable information on their culture.

There was certainly no other tribe in South America about which less was known in proportion to what had been published. Part of this situation was due to certain aspects of Jívaro culture, particularly the making of *tsantsa*, which lent themselves to sensationalistic articles and popular books which were typically based upon a minimum or even an absence of actual contact with the Jívaro. Only two serious major works on them existed: the late Rafael Karsten's *Head-hunters of Western Amazonas* (1935), and M. W. Stirling's *Historical and Ethnographical Material on the Jivaro Indians* (1938). Yet much of what Karsten wrote was vague and highly opinionated, and Stirling's field data were fairly limited due to the short time he spent with the Jívaro. In addition, where the two authors overlapped in subject matter, their reports tended to be strongly contradictory.[1]

In view of this situation, I took both Karsten's and Stirling's works into the field with me and reviewed them sentence by sentence with Jívaro informants. Except for Stirling's data on material culture, I found that there was scarcely a paragraph of ethnographic information in either work that could be considered wholly accurate.

In time, it became evident that the erratic quality of information supplied by both anthropologists derived in part from their reliance on white men as interpreters. Karsten depended almost exclusively on Macabeos, the mestizo inhabitants of the village of Macas, for his communication with Indian informants. He also relied on them for second-hand information on Jívaro culture, as I ascertained by talking to Macabeos who had worked for him. I also found that the Macabeos had misconceptions of Jívaro culture which they believed in so strongly that they were willing to argue with the Indians about the latter's own culture. It was not too different in Stirling's case, although much more expectable, since he was able to spend only a few short months with the Jívaro in comparison with Karsten's intermittent work during several years. Stirling's interpreter was Santiago Baca of Méndez, whom I knew personally, and whom on one occasion I tested as an interpreter. Although a fine person, Baca hardly would let an Indian speak before he reinterpreted and expanded what had been said to fit his own preconceptions. The following portion of a letter from Stirling to me, dated June 30, 1962, in response to an article which I had just published on Jívaro soul beliefs,[2] shows the role of Baca in his work. I would like to add that I consider the letter a tribute to Stirling's scholarly integrity:

It is high time that adequate studies are finally being made of this significant group. When I made my rather hasty trip through the Jivaro country in 1930–31, the working conditions were far from ideal. The expedition was badly organized and from the standpoint of the ethnologist we were never able to stay in one place long enough to get proper results. I knew nothing of the Jivaro language, and depended entirely on the interpreter—Santiago Baca—for the esoteric information. What I recorded was what he understood from the informants. He was, incidentally, a political refugee and had lived 2 years with the Jivaro in hiding.

It is interesting to note that most of the Jivaro we encountered at that time insisted that they knew nothing of religious beliefs —that we would have to contact old Anguasha (on the Yaupe [Yaupi] River). We finally did contact him, and he was the source of most of this type of material which I secured. I am sure that he was a good informant—very sincere and desirous of being precise—so the errors were probably the result of misunderstanding by the interpreter, since I tried not to fill in any interpretations of my own. I had Karsten's work with me, and after getting our own material I checked with Karsten's accounts. The Indians would agree with practically none of his ideas, insisting that they had never heard of such a thing. Incidentally, I never learned with which group he worked—a fact which he appeared to keep secret. I assumed that either the Indians with whom he worked had different concepts, or that he possibly supplied interpretations of his own.

It does not seem probable to me that basic changes in fundamental beliefs could take place in 30 years, so I am inclined to agree with you that the errors in my account were the result of wrong interpretation.

Since the purpose of the present book is to provide a broad introduction to Jívaro culture rather than a detailed comparison with earlier publications, the reader will not find specific criticisms of Karsten's and Stirling's data in the following pages. These will be gradually provided in more specialized publications, which will also have the function of focusing on particular aspects of Jívaro life in greater detail. To the specialist who reads this work, however, I wish to say that statements that he finds here implicitly contradicting those of the two other authors may be taken, in fact, as explicit corrections of their accounts. A contradictory account here does not imply ignorance of their material.

Beyond this, of course, is the question of cultural change. First of all, I wish to note that several of my most important elderly informants were already raising families prior to Karsten's initial Jívaro fieldwork in 1916–18 and did not come into substantial first-hand contact with whites until fifteen to twenty years later. The fieldwork by Stirling occurred later, in 1930–31, but as Stirling himself noted above, the basic source of difference with my own material was probably his interpreter. In addition, I made a special effort to secure field data that would reveal those aspects of Jívaro culture that had changed or remained stable during this century, and the final chapter of the book is devoted to that subject.

Informants' accounts were continually cross-checked and contradictions called to their attention individually. An informant, when thus confronted with a contradiction, and with his reputation for knowledge and veracity at stake, generally provided elaborative supporting detail.

Informants were ordinarily well paid for the time they spent. Payment was commonly in the form of black gunpowder, percussion caps, lead shot, glass and metallic beads, and cloth. Near Ecuadorian and missionary settlements, money was used as well. When visiting strange households it was found that a gift of an ounce or two of gunpowder invariably resulted in a friendly stay, since almost all Jívaro men today possess firearms and continually need replenishment of their supplies of ammunition. Leave-taking in the more isolated parts of the tribal territory typically involved assuring the host of my future return and "taking orders" for additional types of trade goods to be brought on the next visit. Thus my host viewed my continued friendship as being to his advantage and an amiable departure always occurred despite the fact that I was often leaving directly (with gunpowder and other goods) for a household or neighborhood with which he was feuding.

My chief mode of communication to obtain detailed information was through interpreters. However, unlike my predecessors, I exclusively used for this purpose Jívaro men who had learned Spanish as a second language at mission stations. I used a variety of interpreters, eventually working mainly with those who had proven themselves the most accurate, reliable and intelligent. As my own knowledge of the language progressed, I was able to check up on much of that which they interpreted, but even before that stage the comparison of different accounts on the same subject by using different interpreters and informants made substantial verification possible. I personally believe that the proper use of first-class interpreters is an excellent field technique, but that it must be done with sophistication involving constant rephrasing of the same questions in different contexts with various interpreters and informants and supplemented by as much participant observation as possible. It seems likely that at least as many errors in ethnographic research can be committed by the fieldworker who is under the delusion that he is "fluent" in the language, and who fails to check his results through interpreters, as by the researcher who recognizes his linguistic limitations and uses trained interpreters with sensible caution and patience.

The research providing the present data was conducted for a total of fourteen field months in 1956–57, 1964 and 1969, primarily in the following river valleys occupied by the Jívaro: the Río Chiguasa; the Río Macuma; the Río Cangaimi; the Río Cusuimi; the Río Mangosiza; and the Río Upano and its tributaries. Except where otherwise stated, the ethnographic data presented here refer to the culture of those Jívaro who in 1956–57 were not yet in regular first-hand contact with Ecuadorians or other whites.

The 1956–57 field investigation was sponsored by the Henry L. and Grace Doherty Charitable Foundation, Inc., of New York, with supplementary grants from the Department of Anthropology and the Museum of Anthropology of the University of California, Berkeley, the American Museum of Natural History, and the American Anthropological Association (Smith, Kline and French Laboratories contract). The organization and study of the collected data upon my return from the field was facilitated by a University Fellowship in Anthropology from the University of California and by a summer grant from the Social Science Research Council.

Fieldwork in the summer of 1964 was carried out under the auspices of the Associates in Tropical Biogeography of the University of California, Berkeley, and the Robert H. Lowie Museum of Anthropology of the same institution. Sponsorship of the 1969 summer investigations was by the American Museum of Natural History, the Columbia University Council for Research in the Social Sciences, and the Columbia University Institute of Latin American Studies.

I am particularly indebted to Professor John H. Rowe of the Department of Anthropology of the University of California, Berkeley, who first called my attention to the inadequacies of the published material on the Jívaro and who supported me in embarking on the initial field research,[3] when others felt that it was too perilous a project. Other colleagues who have been of particular assistance are Robert F. Murphy, James J. Parsons, Robert L. Carneiro and Kenneth Kensinger. My wife, Sandra, my son, James, and my daughter, Teresa, have helped make this work possible in such profound ways that they will probably never fully realize the depth of their contribution.

Ecuadorians and Americans in Ecuador who especially made possible the success of the fieldwork through their friendship and assistance were Dr. Alberto Flores González, Director of the Instituto Ecuatoriano de Antropología y Geografía, Sr. and Sra. Alfredo Costales Samaniego of the same institute, Mr. and Mrs. Ralph Stuck, Mr. and Mrs. Michael Ficke, Mr. and Mrs. Frank Drown, Mr. W. Ferguson and Mr. and Mrs. Eugene Ferguson, and also Dr. Glen Turner of the Summer Institute of Linguistics, who contributed linguistic information on the Jívaro language. Dr. Turner is not to be held responsible, however, for oversimplifications in the orthography used here.

My greatest debt, and one which I can never adequately

acknowledge, is to the innumerable *šuarä* who guided me in my education in their culture. I value very deeply the sensitivity, intelligence, courtesy and hospitality with which they have consistently treated me. I feel no greater affection and respect for any people on earth.

ORTHOGRAPHY

The Jívaro orthography used here assigns these approximate values to the following phonemes:

VOWELS

a   Spanish *a*

e   English *i* in sit

i   Spanish *i* (nasalized when immediately preceding or following n); when immediately preceding a consonant, it is reiterated immediately following the consonant, except in the case of *r* or *s*)

u   Spanish *u*

CONSONANTS

č   Spanish *ch*

g   Spanish *g* (restricted to a few Spanish loan words)

h   English *h*

k   English *k* (sounded like English *g* when immediately following m, n, or ŋ)

m   Spanish *m*, but more palatized and labialized

n   Spanish *n*

ŋ   English *ng* in sing (followed by a hard *g* sound when not the terminal phoneme)

p   Spanish *p* (sounded like an English *b* when immediately following m, n, or ŋ)

r   Spanish *r*

s   Spanish *s*

š   English *sh*

ts   German *z* in Zimmer
t   Spanish *t* (sounded like Spanish *d* when immediately follow-
      ing m, n, or ŋ)
w   English *w* (but sounded like English *v* when adjacent to *i*)
y   Spanish *y*

Unvoiced vowels (restricted to ultimate syllables) are
marked with ‥. Such vowels tend to be voiced when the
words are shouted loudly. Stress is on the penultimate sylla-
ble, unless otherwise noted. Diphthongs are *ai* and *au*.

The orthography is sometimes not adhered to in the case
of tribal names which are now in current usage in Spanish-
language publications in Ecuador, e.g., "Shuara" (*šuarä*), and
"Achuara" (*ačuarä*).

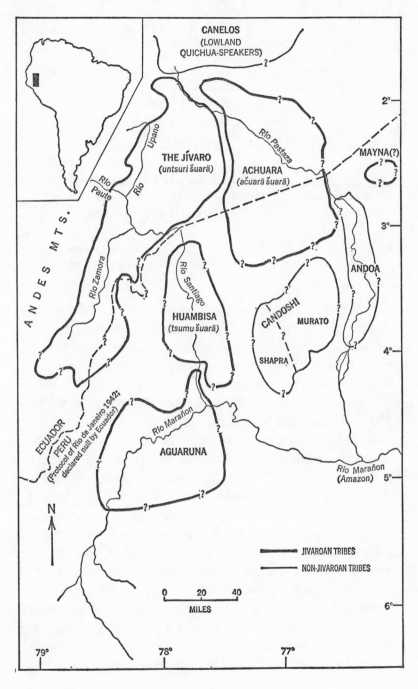

MAP I
Jivaroan and neighboring tribes

Chapter 1

THE JÍVARO: BACKGROUND

I say truly to Your Highnesses that these people are the most insolent that I have seen in all the time that I have traveled in the Indies and engaged in their conquest.

Captain Hernando de Benavente
—on the Jívaro in a letter to
the Royal Audiencia *of Spain,*
March 25, 1550[1]

Where the westward-drifting cloud cover of the upper Amazon basin collides with the eastern cordillera of the Ecuadorian Andes, cold rivulets cascade into the misty forests to form swift, growing streams descending towards the Atlantic Ocean, a continent away. Where the mountain waterfalls give way to rapids, the country of the *untsuri šuarä*, the Jívaro, begins; and where the rapids finally end in placid meandering rivers, so does their homeland. Downstream from the rapids live their traditional enemies, the *ačuarä šuarä* and the *tsumu šuarä*, Indians who travel more by canoe than on foot. But the rapids are more than a geophysical feature; they are a protective barrier that has long halted exploitative penetration of the Jívaro country from the navigable river systems of the rest of the Amazon basin to the east. And the escarpment of the Andes, to their west, which is the most abrupt in all the length of South America, has similarly been an old and silent ally in inhibiting successful conquest and colonization from the highlands. This then, is the home of the Jívaro, a wet, mountainous, and heavily forested sanctuary which helped preserve the freedom and culture of an American Indian tribe more than four hundred years after Cortez and Pizarro.

It is not known how long the Jívaro have dwelt in the forest at the foot of the Andes. Their degree of isolation has been sufficient to make it difficult for most historical linguists[2] to assign Jivaroan dialects and languages (including the now extinct Palta) with certainty to any one of the recognized major language families of South American Indians. However, Greenberg[3] has suggested that Jívaro and Candoshi, along with several other languages, belong to a broad "Andean-Equatorial" family which comprises a great number of languages from northern to southern South America.

Archaeological evidence recovered by the author indicates that at least a portion of the present area occupied by the Jívaro was inhabited by pottery-making (and presumably horticultural) populations at least as early as two and a half millennia ago. Small test excavations in the middle Río Upano Valley, undertaken in 1957, revealed two different ceramic complexes in association with charcoal which provided radiocarbon dates of 609 B.C. ± 440 years and 1041 A.D. ± 160 years.[4] However, the pottery of these two prehistoric complexes is sufficiently different from present-day Jívaro ceramics that it seems difficult to establish a direct cultural connection with certainty. The earlier complex, named "Ipíamais," was discovered southeast of the mestizo village of Huambi in association with artificial earth mounds and ridges, evidence that suggests the possibility of a relatively dense population at that time. The later ceramic complex, termed "Yaunchu," was found near Sucúa and Macas and contained large numbers of specimens of the "red-banded incised" style of pottery recovered in a limited quantity by Collier and Murra[5] in the adjacent highland province of Azuay, which is the source of the Río Paute. It seems clear that the prehistoric populations

residing in the Jívaro region were to some degree, in contact
with the peoples of the Andean highlands.

Today five Jivaroan tribes or dialect groups are known to
inhabit the tropical forest of the Ecuadorian and Peruvian
Amazon: the Jívaro[6]; the Achuara (Atchuara, Achual); the
Huambisa; the Aguaruna; and the "Mayna"[7] (see Map 1).
Of these, the Jívaro, or *untsuri šuarä*, is the best known. This
is the tribe which is usually referred to in the literature and
locally simply as the "Jívaro," "Jíbaro," "Shuar" or "Shuara,"
while the other three Jivaroan tribes are usually locally called
by their special names.

The term "shuara" (*šuarä*) does not simply mean "Jívaro," as has sometimes been said, but means "man," "men"
or "people" and is used by all Jivaroans except the Aguaruna
to refer to any Indian or group of Indians (as opposed to
whites, who are called *apačï*), without regard to cultural or
linguistic affiliation. *Untsuri šuarä*, meaning "numerous Indians," is a more accurate native designation for the Jívaro
proper, which is applied to them by the Achuara (*ačuarä
šuarä*) to the east. An alternative term, *muraiya šuarä* ("hill
Indians") is also applied to the Jívaro proper by the Achuara.
The Huambisa (*tsumu šuarä*) refer to the Jívaro proper as
"*makas šuarä*" or "*yukina šuarä*,"[8] while the Aguaruna call
them the "*patuka širay*."[9] Since the native designations vary,
and are not in common usage in the literature, the practice in
the present study will be simply to use the term "Jívaro"
when referring to this tribe. Other tribes, when mentioned,
will be given their specific names, e.g., Achuara.

The Jívaro population, numbering an estimated 7,830
persons in 1956–57,[10] dwells chiefly between the Río Pastaza
in the north, and the upper Río Zamora in the south; and
from about 1,200 meters altitude above sea level on the
eastern slope of the Andes in the west to the Río Pangui

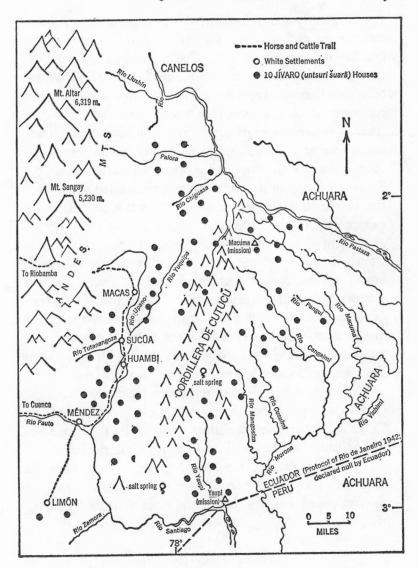

MAP 2

Distribution of the Jívaro, or *untsuri šuarä*,
north of the Río Zamora in 1956–57

(approximately 400 meters altitude) in the east. Map 2 shows most of the region except for the southern extension along and beyond the Río Zamora. The tribal territory north of the Río Santiago is bisected by the rugged, jungle-clad Cordillera de Cutucú, which runs roughly north and south and reaches an altitude of more than 2,000 meters above sea level. There are settlements of Ecuadorian colonists in the Jívaro territory west of the Cordillera de Cutucú in the Upano and Paute valleys and also southwest of the cordillera in the Zamora Valley, but the mountain range has acted as an effective barrier to white settlement in the lands inhabited by the eastern part of the tribe.

Most of the Jívaro dwelling west of the Cordillera de Cutucú and south of the Río Chiguasa region are in continuous first-hand contact with the frontier of Ecuadorian settlement and are here called the "frontier Jívaro."[11] Those beyond the frontier of Ecuadorian colonization—the object of this study—are mainly east of the Cutucú range and are sometimes referred to here as the "interior Jívaro," since the region is locally known, in Spanish, as "adentro."

The northern neighbors of the Jívaro are the Canelos (also locally known as the "Alama," "Quichua" [Quechua] or "Yumbo"), who speak a dialect of Inca. To the east dwell the Achuara Jivaroans, and to the south along the Río Santiago and Río Morona, the Huambisa Jivaroans.[12] Thus the Jívaro are bounded on the west by an Ecuadorian white or mestizo population, and on the other three sides by native tribes.

Jívaro-White Contacts

Prior to the Spanish Conquest, the Jívaro were bounded on the west by the Inca Empire, which had conquered all the highland Ecuadorian groups, such as the Cañari, adjacent to the Jívaro region. Shortly before the arrival of the Spaniards on the Ecuadorian coast in 1527, the Inca emperor, Huayna Capac, led an army to conquer the Jivaroans (probably Jívaro or Aguaruna) inhabiting the region known as "Bracamoros." The invasion, which probably took place in the drainages of the upper Zamora and Chinchipe rivers, was met by such fierce resistance that Huayna Capac had to flee ignominiously back to the Andean highlands, attempting to placate his pursuers with gifts as he retreated. According to one account, he claimed that he would avenge himself on them. According to another version, he explained away his failure by declaring that the inhabitants of Bracamoros were unworthy of being his subjects.[13]

The first reported white penetration of Jívaro territory was made in 1549 by a Spanish expedition commanded by Hernando de Benavente. Probably descending the eastern slopes of the Andes from the headwaters of the Río Upano, Benavente and his men appear to have followed this river southward to its junction with the Río Paute. There they encountered a people living in the "land and province of Xívaro," dwelling in houses scattered more than a league apart. Benavente had planned to establish a town there, but found the Jívaro too hostile and their environment too disagreeable to establish a settlement. He shortly beat a retreat back to the Ecuadorian highlands.[14]

The Viceroy of Peru soon sent a new expedition of colonists, as well as soldiers, into the Jívaro territory. These newcomers engaged in trade with the Indians,[15] made peace pacts with them, and began to exploit the rich placer gold deposits of the Paute, Zamora and Upano rivers and their tributaries. Experiencing great success in their gold mining activities, the Spaniards founded two major communities, described as "cities," in 1552: Logroño, possibly at the junction of the Río Paute (and Río Upano) with the Río Zamora; and Sevilla del Oro, probably somewhere on the middle Río Upano.[16]

Although the Spaniards were evidently able to obtain the co-operation of some Jívaro in working the placer deposits, others were hostile. Juan Aldrete reported in 1582:

They [the Jívaro] are a very warlike people, and have killed a great number of Spaniards, and are killing them every day. It is a very rough land, having many rivers and canyons, all of which in general have gold and in such quantity that the Spaniards are obliged to forget the danger and try to subject them for the profits which they can obtain and which the land promises.[17]

As the Spaniards subjected the Jívaro, they required tribute in gold dust, and increased their demands as the years progressed.[18] Finally, in 1599, the Spaniards' demands culminated in the famous Jívaro uprising described by Velasco:

The cause of this tragedy is attributed above all else to the excessive greed of the last Governor of Macas; and the opportune occasion for carrying it out was the celebrations of the coronation of Philip III of Spain. In order to understand such a memorable event, one first has to presuppose several points:

(1) That the Indian nations of this [regional] government for the most part still remained, even if not completely, idolatrous and heathenish; because there were here so few men of the Church, laymen as well as priests, who had hardly begun to develop something more than a parish of Indians.

(2) That the Jíbaro nation, very widely spread through many regions, was not conquered . . . except only in part, the main body of the nation remaining without bridle or yoke, scattered in the immense regions of the Morona and its tributary rivers and lakes.

(3) That the conquered inhabitants of the Paute, where the city of Logroño was founded, remained very displeased with the unequal administration of its taxes, done because of their old rebelliousness.

(4) That even though they were paid for their labor, in iron tools and other goods, in accordance with the ordinances of President LaGasca, that immediate inducement did not offset their innate idleness, and they worked the gold mines with much reluctance.

Given these points, it is easy to understand with how much activity the uprising would be prepared. Above all, it is necessary to understand that the Jíbaros of the Morona, who were the leaders, had renewed their friendship and alliance with those of the Paute, in the interest of having, through them, the iron tools that they needed.

With the matters of government in these critical circumstances, there arrived orders from the royal Audiencia that there, as everywhere, they conduct the customary ceremony of the oath of allegiance to the King. The Governor, who did not miss an opportunity to enrich himself, wanted to take advantage of this. He proclaimed an edict in the capital, and had it announced in all the [regional] government through his lieutenants, fixing the day well in advance, and imposing a large tax, under the name of a gift, for the solemn royal celebrations, he being the one having to go out to collect it in person in the three provinces, equally from the Spaniards as from the Indians.

As soon as this order was proclaimed, rebellion was also proclaimed in all the [regional] governments, with the greater activity among the Spaniards than among the Indians. Since they [the Spaniards] knew the purpose of asking such a big gift, they resolved to pay the cost of the celebrations themselves, although it might cost more, in order not to enrich the Governor by putting it into his hands. They spoke openly and resolutely about the case, and afraid of not being heard, they elected in their meetings several leaders of a formal and declared conspiracy against the injustice of the order. The Governor, fearing its effects, since all the Spaniards were stirred up, explained to them, by himself privately, that the gift was free and voluntary, and that each should only contribute according to his means. But he did not explain nor intimate this to the Indians; as a result, while the Spaniards had calmed down, the Indians remained upset.

The Macas and Huamboyas submitted to the order with resignation. The Jíbaros entered into many consultations, and already were resolved to throw off the yoke, retreating to the Morona. Seeing them with this determination, Quirruba [*Kirupasa?* ("Big Frog")], chief of one of their settlements, very alert and capable, quieted them all down. He told them that that was not the sure way of liberating themselves permanently from the Christians: that if they were attempting to do that, they must entrust themselves to his direction, and must bind themselves to execute in secret all that which he would order, and not to think, for then, of making a withdrawal.

They accepted his proposition and swore to recognize him as their leader and liberator. He imposed two obligations upon them: first, inviolate secrecy on which everything depended; and second, that they seek not only the gold that the Governor ordered, but whatever more they were able to, in order that this might be the price of their liberty, feigning to seek gold with great enthusiasm to solemnize the royal celebrations.

Meanwhile, Quirruba asked, through messengers, for aid from all of the Jíbaros of the Morona; and having it assured, he insisted on involving the Macas and Huamboyas in the same conspiracy by means of secret emissaries, because his plan was to wipe out all the Spaniards of the [regional] government at the same time on the same day. He learned the day which the Governor had fixed for his arrival in Logroño, where Quirruba himself was to go personally with part of the army.

He designated two others in whom he had confidence as leaders of the undertaking: one for the capital of Sevilla del Oro, and the other for the town of Huamboya, in order that each one, aided by the local Indians and by the troops of Jíbaros that were distributed in those parts, that all might become blood and fire. The fear of being destroyed by the Jíbaros caused the two faint-hearted nations of Macas and Huamboyas to agree to the resolved plan; but only in appearance, and without intention to co-operate in the massacre, except to keep the secret and to put all of themselves out of danger.

The fatal day came with the arrival of the Governor at Logroño, without any aspect of the conspiracy having leaked out up to then. The Spaniards slept quite without worry in the unfortunate city when it was taken cautiously, at midnight, by the enemy army. This exceeded 20,000 Indians, according to recorded report, outside of the troops who had already marched to Sevilla and to Huamboya. Surrounding the city, they invaded and occupied all of its sections simultaneously, so that the Spaniards would not be able to unite, and they were forced to die in their own homes.

The principal chief, Quirruba, who had carried out all of the preparations with great cunning, took possession of the house in which the Governor was staying. Surrounding the house, Quirruba entered it with sufficient troops, carrying all the gold that his nation had amassed for the celebrations; and at the same time the implements for melting it. They killed all the people who were inside, except for the Governor, who was in a state of undress because of the surprise. They told him that it was now time for him to receive the tax of gold which he had ordered prepared.

They stripped him completely naked, tied his hands and feet; and while some amused themselves with him, delivering a thousand castigations and jests, the others set up a large forge in the courtyard, where they melted the gold. When it was ready in the crucibles, they opened his mouth with a bone, saying that they wanted to see if for once he had enough gold. They poured it little by little, and then forced it down with another bone; and bursting his bowels with the torture, all raised a clamor and laughter.

With the completion of this horrible sacrifice around dawn,

all of the city was also finished, without scarcely a single man escaping. The encirclement was maintained until the next day, when they extinguished the torches of copal that had burned in all the streets and houses. While they searched for those in hiding, and looted all that they were able to carry, they sent part of the army to the other two cities, in case more help was needed.

Of all the females they had spared, they killed the old and the very young who could only be a burden, and saved the rest for their use. Among this number were almost all of the nuns of a monastery of the Conception founded a few years earlier, because except for the old women who founded it, the rest were young. Before midday they received the news that nothing had been carried out against the capital, because of the failure of the Macas to keep their word. Therefore, they sent more troops, leaving in Logroño those necessary to guard the females and the booty, and to complete the ruin by burning the houses one by one.

In the capital of Sevilla del Oro, 25 leagues distant, neither was the conspiracy discovered until the morning of the same fatal day. The Macas, being cowards, or rather being loyal to the Spaniards, did not resolve to co-operate; but neither did they have the courage to reveal the secret in time, out of fear of their mortal enemies. Those who were somewhat distant from the capital retired to the forests before the appointed day, and some of those closest to the capital fled into the city with their families, food and belongings, saying that they had learned that the Jíbaros of the Morona were going to destroy the cities and settlements of the government that night; because of that it was necessary for the Spaniards to be called to arms and to prepare a defense.

The number of inhabitants of the capital was great, but the major part useless in the situation, and could only serve as a hindrance. They had many weapons put away since the Conquest, but without maintenance and with very little gunpowder: the cavalry was almost nonexistent, because it was useless in the country: the consternation was excessive; because each one was thinking more of saving his family and possessions than of the common defense, it was difficult to conduct it to advantage: nevertheless, the city and royal officials tried hard to make as much preparation as was possible, intrenching the streets, and placing those under arms in the locations of the most danger, not having forces or preparation for a battle outside the city. The officials transported all of the royal treasury and its boxes to the main church, fortifying it as a citadel and final refuge. They also fortified the church of the nuns of the Conception, cramming into it all of the women and children. At nightfall, a portion of the inhabitants of the town of Huamboya, 16 leagues distant, entered the city, having sent all of the rest to Riobamba and its environs. All of these fled, abandoning their houses and goods, because at dawn that day they learned, from a lone sick Indian who had remained, that all the people of his nation had retreated to the Cordillera de Cubillin, fleeing the Jíbaros, who were going to destroy everyone that night.

They rejoiced in Sevilla del Oro with the recruitment of those people, and passed all the night on watch, awaiting the enemy. Seeing that they neither appeared the next day, they began to doubt the existence of the conspiracy. They thus won time to complete the defense somewhat more, to bring in a supply of food from the neighboring countryside, and to gather the Spaniards sprinkled in the mining camps and small settlements of the district.

The reason that the barbarians postponed the appointed time by 24 hours was because the Macas, who were summoned to join with them and to lead them, as guides, to the city, did not appear at their appointed meeting place. Finding the Macas to be unfaithful, they delayed the march, and sent word to Logroño to supply more troops. These arrived between midnight and dawn the next day, and together they marched against Sevilla del Oro, burning with desire to avenge themselves, not so much against the Spaniards, as against the Macas Indians, for having broken their promise.

The Spaniards worked themselves up into going forth onto the adjacent plain to see if they could stop the invasion of the city, which the barbarians surrounded at daybreak, as conquerors and proclaiming a victory ahead of time. They were received with a volley that made them halt their advance. The initial impetus was checked for a while because of the many dead; later, observing that the shots of the guns, the only weapons they feared, were continually becoming less frequent, and knowing that the Spaniards were short on powder, they made bold so that, wielding their lances, they compelled the Spaniards to retreat to the trenches of the city.

The Jíbaros did not fear the swords, pikes, or lances, protected by a kind of buckler and very strong round shields. All day they made so many assaults of such a furious nature that, fighting hand to hand, they succeeded in piercing the trenches and in taking possession of almost all of the city. The confusion and massacre of thousands grew here and there in various small battles in the streets and plazas, until with the arrival of night the barbarians were satisfied to set fire to many portions of the city, and to make their withdrawal.

One Jíbaro, unable to follow the rest because he had lost both legs, was found among the dead. This was the only person through whom it was known afterward that which has been recounted with regard to the conspiracy and tragedy of Logroño: because he was one of those being from that same city, who helped in the sacrifice of the unfortunate Governor. It was not known then or later what the Jíbaros did in the town of Mendoza, not finding in it either Spaniards or Indians.

Neither could it be known with certainty the number of dead in the two cities. It appears by the minimum calculation that in Logroño they did not exceed more than 12 thousand inhabitants of all kinds and ages, because it was a medium-sized city; but of all of them none was spared except the serviceable women, who would have preferred to have died than to be carried off as captives by the barbarians. Of the capital of Sevilla del Oro, which is on record as having been large and populous, with more than 25 thousand inhabitants, between citizens and merchants from the outside, it is said that not a fourth remained, this being almost all women and children, with very few men.

Upon the pitiful fall of this government [of Macas], the total ruin of the territory of Yaguarzongo followed as a consequence, and the almost total ruin of Jaén, of which I shall tell you in due time; and that of Loja and Quijos, which I have already reported. Even the highest and most secure provinces of the Kingdom [of Quito] experienced notable unrest on the part of the peoples upon notification of the horrendous catastrophe: it reached even to the barbaric nations of Popayan, and caused them, by its bad example, to commit the insolences and destructions to which I referred in speaking of its cities.

It was a special providence of Heaven that at nightfall the triumphant barbarians unexpectedly withdrew from Sevilla del Oro, the reason being unknown, they being able to have easily consummated the slaughter of everyone. The wretched remnant, informed of all that had happened in Logroño, remained fearing the return of the barbarians at any moment; and no longer capable of resistance, they only thought of saving themselves. Small parties of children and women, with an occasional man, were leaving on foot with a thousand hardships, and without any food, to take refuge in other cities of the Kingdom; and not a single person would have stayed, if an opportune relief had not shortly arrived from Quito.[19]

Those Spaniards who stayed retreated north to the upper Río Upano Valley and founded the refugee settlement of Macas. Some years later these people of Macas (commonly referred to as Macabeos) made sorties southward to mine the old placer gold deposits, but apparently these attempts ended in failure, due to attacks by the Jívaro.[20]

From 1599 until almost the middle of the nineteenth century, the Jívaro apparently had only intermittent and generally hostile contacts with whites. Some missionary and military expeditions entered the region from the Andean highlands, but several ended disasterously and none of them resulted in permanent colonization.[21] One of the few "friendly" gestures reported for the tribe during this time occurred in 1767, when they gave a Spanish missionizing expedition "gifts," which included the skulls of Spaniards who had apparently been killed earlier by the Jívaro.[22]

Interestingly, the present-day Jívaro seem to have no memory of their uprising of 1599. The only oral tradition that I was able to obtain which apparently concerned the Spaniards was this, from one of my oldest informants:

A very long time ago there were the *ai apači* ["*ai*" white men]. They were many. They were all of bone to their elbows and to their knees. They could move their arms and legs only beyond their elbows and knees. They had shirts and pants. They were fierce and tall. There were many, many of them, and they had women and children. All were the same in not being able to move except for their forearms and lower legs. They didn't have hats, but wore something like the helmets of the [present-day Ecuadorian] soldiers. These men had machetes of iron that they used for killing. They carried their machetes on the left hip. The machetes were somewhat yellow. These machetes had handles of human bone. They said that they had killed many whites with their machetes. They also had shoes. These whites had *mačiu* . . . they rode on top of these. I think these must have been horses. The *šuarä* were scared of them. These whites also had *mua*. I do not know what they were.

The informant explained that the bone extending to the knees and elbows of the *ai apači* was something like the shell of a turtle. It seems evident that he was recounting a tradition concerning men in armor and helmets and carrying swords. Since they had shoes, the informant discounted the possibility that they were Macabeos, since the latter "did not have shoes." The *maču* whom the informant thought must be horses are clearly he-mules (Spanish: *macho*). The *mua* for which he could not suggest an identity undoubtedly are she-mules (Spanish: *mula*), since the Jívaro have difficulty pronouncing *l*. In view of the fact that "many, many" whites are referred to, including women and children, this account may actually concern the sixteenth-century occupation by the Spaniards. It is remarkable, however, that the informant had no information as to whether the Jívaro fought the *ai apači*, although he thought it was possible.

From 1599 to 1870, Macas remained the only permanent white settlement near the Jívaro. This little community was linked to the outside world by means of a single foot trail to the highland city of Riobamba. There is even one Macabeo tradition that for some time after the 1599 uprising the people of Macas "lost" the trail and were completely cut off from the outside world. While the truth of this particular tradition is dubious, it does illustrate the Macabeos' sense of isolation. By the early nineteenth century, however, Macabeo men were regularly using the trail to make the sixteen-day round trip hike to Riobamba to obtain machetes, axes, cloth, needles, and firearms for their remote community.

The Jívaro apparently launched attacks repeatedly in the seventeenth and eighteenth century from the Río Paute region, forcing the Macabeos to relocate their village several times. The people of Macas, unlike the Jívaro, had a few firearms, and this advantage, it is believed by them, contributed importantly to their survival.[23] The Macabeos and Jívaro were still fighting in 1837, but by the mid-nineteenth century peaceful trade relations had been initiated between the two groups.[24]

The Jívaro have an oral tradition regarding the circumstances of the initiation of this peaceful contact:

In the old days, all the Jívaro [*untsuri šuarä*] lived near the Río Paute. Then two Jívaro went up the Río Upano Valley and found many monkeys. Near the Río Tutanangoza, they encountered two Macabeos, who wore kilts like the *šuarä*, but carried machetes. The Macabeos spoke a Jivaroan dialect different from theirs [Achuara?]. The Macabeos asked, "Do you have pigs?" The Jívaro men said, "Yes." So the Macabeos gave one of the Jívaro a piece of a machete blade and told him to bring pigs to Macas. The two *šuarä* returned downstream and told their people:

"We have encountered an animal, or perhaps it is a person, who wears a kilt. It gave us this machete."

All the people tried out the machete blade fragment, happy with how well it worked compared to their stone axes. So they killed a few big pigs and gave the meat to some old women to carry to Macas. Two men went with the old women on the trail, but did not enter Macas with them. They were afraid of the whites, and thought that perhaps they would kill them. The men waited on the trail for the old women to return.

When the women arrived in Macas with the meat, the whites gave them a shirt, four arm lengths of cloth to make a dress, and one piece of machete. One of the old women later said when she returned home, "They frightened me because they have such large houses and so many people."

After two days, the old women came back down the trail, surprising their people, who had decided that they had been killed. The old women told them that the Macabeos had many machetes and much cloth which they wanted to exchange for pigs.

So, after a few days, four men left for Macas, carrying pigs. When they arrived, the whites sat them on stools and served them beer of sugar cane. The Macabeos gave the men two machetes, two hatchets, and cloth. Following this, the Macabeos returned the visit of the *šuarä*.

With this initiation of trade relations between the two groups, Jívaro families soon migrated north from the Río Paute Valley to settle in the previously uninhabited land between the Río Paute and Macas. These migrants began to act as middlemen in the barter of Jívaro products for steel machetes and other goods. The Macabeos at first traded mainly to secure pigs and salt obtained by the Jívaro from saline springs, but soon also began to attend *tsantsa* celebrations to purchase lard obtained from pigs slaughtered by the Jívaro on such occasions. As a consequence of their attendance at the feasts, the Macabeos started also to purchase *tsantsa*.[25] This was the beginning of the "shrunken head" trade, and the first reported examples of *tsantsa* reached the outside world at about this time.[26]

Macas remained the only significant source of Western-manufactured goods for the Jívaro until 1870. In that year, the Jesuits founded new missions at Macas and Gualaquiza, to the south on the Río Zamora.[27] The Jesuit missionaries introduced the first cattle to Macas at this time, Macabeo men carrying calves and guinea grass (*gramalote* in Spanish) sets on their backs down the long trail from Riobamba. Both cattle and the grass flourished, and soon the Macabeos had a plentiful supply of beef, with the result that a gradual decline occurred in the trade with the Jívaro for pigs. Being unable to barter pigs any longer to obtain steel tools and other trade goods, the Jívaro began to engage in labor, such as clearing forest for pastures, for the people of Macas.

The Jesuits were shortly forced to withdraw from Guala-quiza and Macas due to political reasons, but they left behind them at Gualaquiza a few mestizos who constituted the first new permanent white settlement in the Jívaro region since 1599. These mestizos seem to have been tolerated by the Jívaro as a source of Western-manufactured goods, especially machetes and steel lance heads, the latter specially manufactured in the adjacent highland province of Azuay for the Jívaro trade.

In 1887, the Dominican order founded a Catholic mission at Macas, but abandoned it in 1898 without apparently having had much effect on the Jívaro.[28] A Protestant mission of the Gospel Missionary Union was established at Macas in 1902, but it likewise was soon terminated.[29]

The last two decades of the century were also marked by visits to Macas by gatherers of cinchona bark and rubber. These commercial collectors generally employed Macabeos as guides and intermittently bartered guns and other trade goods to the Jívaro in exchange for latex or other natural products. However, the rubber trade existed only in an attenuated form in this remote portion of the Amazon, partly because of the problem of transporting the rubber in the absence of navigable rivers.

Although the Amazon rubber boom soon began to decline, other new inroads into the western Jívaro territory were shortly made by the Catholic Salesians, who founded missions at Méndez, near the juncture of the Río Paute and Río Upano, in 1914, and then at Macas in 1924.[30] Except for these missionaries, however, white colonization of the region was still slight. Even Macas remained so isolated from the outside world that the first horse was not brought into the village until 1928, when a man carried a colt on his back from Riobamba, according to local informants.

In 1932, Macas was described by a visitor as follows:

Macas stands in the midst of a highly fertile district, and is really a group of small farms supporting about five hundred people. Its fine cattle are known, by hearsay at least, throughout Ecuador, but it is rarely that any are driven up to the markets of the plateau. The long trail to Riobamba, the only route from the village to the plateau, is at all seasons of the year so deep in mud that cattle cannot stand the journey over it. One wonders, indeed, how and why such a settlement as Macas exists. But it must be borne in mind that the inhabitants, as in certain sections of eastern Bolivia, Colombia, and Peru, as well, are of a type of which white men elsewhere can scarcely conceive. They are with few exceptions a people so long reduced, because of their inability to engage in trade of any importance, to a state in which they have no desires that cannot be satisfied by the land on which they live. Shelter and food are their chief wants. The few articles of their monotonous diet are easily grown. Their huts of bamboo slats . . . are easily constructed from material immediately at hand. On their infrequent trips to the plateau, they may carry with them a bit of gold washed from a nearby stream, a little crude alcohol distilled from cane grown on a river playa, a few homemade cigars, a little coffee or cacao, wherewith to purchase a few yards of cheap cloth needed for clothing. Their life is easy, tranquil and even plentiful within their conception of plenty. The region could undoubtedly support many more people in such a state of plenty and tranquility, but such a life could scarcely satisfy the desirable type of colonist, either local or foreign, who breaks old ties and traditions to set out to find a better life in new lands.[31]

Even as the above sketch was being published, however, a new wave of white colonists had begun to enter this western part of the Jívaro territory.[32] Mestizo workers who had accompanied the Salesian missionaries to Méndez were rediscovering the rich placer gold deposits which the Spaniards had mined in the sixteenth century on the lower Río Paute, lower Río Zamora, and lower Río Upano. Ecuadorians from the province of Azuay in the adjoining Andean highlands soon came down in large numbers to try their luck at gold mining. Unlike their sixteenth-century predecessors, they did not usually attempt to coerce the Jívaro as conquerors, but came as individual prospector-miners. The fact that the Jívaro were fairly well equipped with firearms by this time,[33] probably contributed to this situation. When conflicts with the Jívaro occurred, they were usually settled, one way or another, directly by the individuals involved.

The gold rush reached its peak in 1937, at which time the boom town of Méndez seems to have approached a population of about three thousand—far above that of Macas. Shortly, however, a decline in mining profits took place, and many of the white prospector-miners returned to the highlands. Others remained to settle permanently in the Upano, Paute, and Zamora valleys.

During these gold rush years, the first horse trail had been built into the Jívaro region, connecting the highland province of Azuay with Méndez, and after the boom was over, the trail was kept open by the Salesian missionaries. Gradually, Azuay mestizos, some of them ex-miners, began to immigrate into the region with their families to raise cattle, which they could then drive out over the trail to the city of Cuenca to obtain cash. The local Jívaro at first generally welcomed the settlers as a new source of factory-manufactured goods, particularly machetes and muzzle-loading shotguns, which they received for clearing the forest to make pastures for the colonists' cattle.

Cattle raising proved successful, and soon more colonists arrived. As their numbers increased and they were augmented by military and police units, their fear of the Jívaro diminished, and they began seizing the Indians' garden clearings for pastures. The Jívaro say that over half of their Upano Valley population also died at this time of epidemics of contagious diseases carried by the colonists and that this depopulation greatly facilitated the seizure of Jívaro gardens by the whites. As the frontier of the white settlement pushed inexorably up the Río Upano Valley in the direction of Macas, many Jívaro lost their lands to the new immigrants, and often fled eastward across the Cordillera de Cutucú, or moved northward to the Río Chiguasa region.

Around 1941, Jívaro-white relations became extremely tense due to the war between Peru and Ecuador. Ecuadorian troops attacked a Jívaro neighborhood near the Río Santiago reportedly because they believed that the Indians were from Peru and led by Peruvian army officers. In the resulting bloodshed, seventy-seven Ecuadorians and an unknown number of Jívaro, including women and children, were reportedly killed. The other Jívaro began to fear that the Ecuadorians planned to exterminate all of them to get their lands. Almost all the Jívaro neighborhoods along the frontier of Ecuadorian colonization rapidly called a truce among themselves and made secret plans to conduct a co-ordinated revolt at the first sign of a general attack by the Ecuadorians. Elaborate strategic plans and tactical assignments were agreed upon by the leading warriors of the normally feuding neighborhoods. Undoubtedly the mechanics of making this emergency alliance were very similar to those involved in the destruction of the Spaniards in 1599. However, the planned revolt never was initiated because the expected Ecuadorian offensive against the Jívaro did not occur.

A few years later, the Salesian missionaries persuaded the government of Ecuador to set aside certain lands in the Upano Valley as church-administered reservations for use by missionized Jívaro. Protestant evangelist missionaries also subsequently obtained a small land grant for a similar purpose in the same valley, around 1950. Today almost all the frontier

Jívaro reside in such mission-administered lands, since Ecuadorian settlers have taken over almost all of the remainder of the desirable land in the Upano Valley. New white settlements which have sprung up in the Río Upano frontier region include Sucúa (by the Río Tutanangoza), Huambi, Huambinimi, and Logroño (the latter three between Sucúa and Méndez) (see Map 2). By 1950, the reported white population in the Río Upano frontier region had reached 1,811 persons, as against 2,356 Jívaro in the same valley.[84]

By 1956, the Jívaro west of the Cordillera de Cutucú were largely in direct, continuous contact with the Spanish-speaking Ecuadorian population. In this frontier zone, white soldiers and police had imposed the national laws on the Jívaro. White settlers had seized almost all of the land except that protected by the missionaries, and employed the Jívaro in wage labor. Missionaries, with the backing of law enforcement agencies, were putting the Jívaro children in boarding schools and enculturating them to the new, alien way of life. This direct, unremitted contact was tending to acculturate the frontier Jívaro to the national Ecuadorian way of life and the direction of the trend was towards eventual assimilation.

The Interior Jívaro

In contrast, the Jívaro beyond the frontier of colonization still were not yet in continuous first-hand contact with the white population at the time of the investigator's original fieldwork in 1956–57, and these are the people whose culture will be described here. Their territory, mainly east of the Cordillera de Cutucú, had been rarely, if ever, penetrated by any Spanish expedition or later group of Ecuadorian colonizers. This mountain barrier, which is traversed by an arduous journey of two or more days on foot, still discourages white penetration into the eastern interior.

Cases of contact between the interior Jívaro and whites are all very recent and highly localized in their occurrence. The largest intrusion was made by the Royal Dutch Shell Oil Corporation in the early 1940's as part of an ill-fated oil exploration project. The company constructed a small airstrip near the Río Pangui in the easternmost part of the Jívaro territory, but within a few years abandoned the site altogether when explorations failed to reveal economically exploitable oil deposits in the region. The project involved relatively limited interaction with the Jívaro.

In 1945, a North American evangelist missionary belonging to the Gospel Missionary Union established a small outpost on the middle Río Macuma. The mission has a small airstrip supplied by single-engine plane since 1946. A subsidiary airstrip was built on the upper Río Cangaimi at the end of 1954.[35] At the time of the investigator's first fieldwork, the Macuma mission was beginning to exert some significant influence on the Jívaro families residing at the mission, but such contacts were still limited to the immediate locality, without any noticeable effect on the culture of the other Jívaro inhabiting the vast interior region east of the Cordillera de Cutucú. The Salesians had also founded a mission on the lower Río Yaupi, with similar localized effects.

Localities within the interior Jívaro territory which had been least touched by white contact in 1956–57 are the ones from which the data are primarily drawn for the present study. These areas include: the upper Río Cangaimi; the upper Río Cusuimi; the upper Río Mangosiza; and the region between the Río Chiguasa and the headwaters of the Río Yuquipa and the Río Macuma (see Map 2). The last region is west of the northern end of the Cutucú mountain barrier but was still largely isolated from colonists' incursions by the swift, bridgeless Río Upano and its often deep canyon (see Plate 1), which acted as an obstacle throughout its length to eastward migration by the horse-dependent settlers. These localities (excluding missions and their environs) had, together with other areas of minimal white penetration, an estimated total population of approximately 2,205 persons. Beginning with Chapter II, the present tense will be used to describe interior Jívaro culture as it existed at the time of the original fieldwork. In other words, the "ethnographic present" is 1956–57.

Whether this population in the northern and eastern portion of the tribe was larger or smaller than in previous decades is difficult to determine in the absence of written records. It does appear, however, that three of the localities involved, the Río Chiguasa region, the middle Río Macuma area, and the Río Yaupi Valley, were not occupied by the Jívaro until around the turn of the century. These occupations were the consequence of head-taking raids by the Jívaro which forced the Achuara (ačuarä šuarä) to retreat northeastward from the Chiguasa and middle Macuma areas and the Huambisa (tsumu šuarä) to withdraw southward from the Yaupi region. This territorial expansion by the Jívaro was a by-product, rather than a conscious purpose, of their tsantsa raids against these adjacent tribes.[36]

Once vacated, such formerly enemy-held regions attracted Jívaro from the Río Upano Valley, elderly untsuri šuarä informants explained, because the hunting and fishing were better than in the Upano area. The superior hunting and fishing were also given as the reason that families had, for decades at least, moved eastward across the Cordillera de Cutucú to join their tribesmen already settled there. Later, when white colonists entered the Upano Valley in large numbers from the highland province of Azuay in the 1930's, many more Jívaro families migrated eastward to escape harassment. Thus it seems evident that the population of the interior Jívaro has been substantially augmented by migration for at least a century.

The picture is less clear with regard to the demographic effects of disease upon the interior Jívaro. Epidemics of contagious disease, especially measles and whooping cough, appear to have had devastating effects in the twentieth century among these people. Informants claim that in some cases half of the populations of their neighborhoods were wiped out in a single epidemic. It is difficult to evaluate such statements, but they are not inconsistent with what we know of the effects of such diseases on other South American forest Indians under observation at times when they were struck by measles and smallpox. In addition, common colds and similar respiratory ailments easily reach epidemic proportions among the Jívaro, with complications of a fatal nature being common, especially among infants and the elderly. The fear of colds is so great that it can act as a barrier to acceptance of the anthropological fieldworker, who must, of course, take every precaution to be sure that he and his companions are not, in fact, bringing the disease.

Malaria is endemic, but is recognized by elderly informants as being an anciently introduced disease "brought by Jívaro coming back from Peru." The Jívaro believe that it is transmitted when sharing the bowl in which manioc beer is served. It would seem highly likely that malaria, an Old World disease, which possibly has been present among the Jívaro since the sixteenth century, has had substantial effects on their rate of mortality and thus upon their long-range population size and density. Again, however, the lack of relevant written records makes it almost impossible to judge its actual demographic effects.

Informants report that a significant new disease in the interior is gonorrhea, which they say was brought to the Upano Valley Jívaro by Colombians during the rubber boom at the beginning of this century and has only recently crossed the Cutucú range. The Colombians were also said to have brought mumps. Interestingly, although smallpox epidemics are known in the Upano region, the interior Jívaro east of the Cordillera de Cutucú do not recall the disease ever having spread to them. Tuberculosis is said to have been completely unknown anywhere in the Jívaro country until the colonists from Azuay moved in, but is now common.

The demographic trends among the interior Jívaro thus are sketchy and conflicting. On the one hand, there has been a definite growth through in-migration from the Upano Valley in the face of the advancing white population; but on the other hand, a high incidence of mortality has apparently occurred, especially among the very young and the elderly, as a result of serious epidemics of introduced contagious disease. Another imponderable demographic factor is the shift that has occurred during the past half-century from large-scale headhunting wars with other tribes, in which men, women, and children were all killed, to an emphasis on individual assassination within the tribe directed primarily at adult males. Given the various conflicting trends and uncertainties involved, about all that seems clear is that there is no obvious overall trend of population growth or decline among the interior Jívaro during the first half of the twentieth century. The area occupied by them, however, does seem to have expanded.

In addition to the Río Upano and the Cutucú mountain

barriers, intra-tribal feuding between neighborhoods has contributed significantly to the insulation of the interior Jívaro from contact with the frontier whites. Internal hostilities have discouraged many men from traveling more than ten or fifteen miles from their homes. Many have not been willing to risk traveling that far, for fear of assassination by personal enemies or enemies of close relatives. At the time of the author's original fieldwork in 1956–57, such fears produced a situation in which relatively few of the men deep in the interior had even briefly visited the region of Ecuadorian colonization.

The relative isolation of the interior Jívaro, however, had not prevented them from obtaining increasing quantities of machetes, steel axes, and shotguns. By means of neighborhood-to-neighborhood relays of native trading partners, these products of Western civilization were passed from the frontier Jívaro into the most remote parts of the tribal territory. All of the interior Jívaro neighborhoods were thus supplied with steel cutting tools, firearms, and ammunition without the necessity of coming into direct contact with the white population.

The growth of this trade in recent decades had been made possible by the increasing involvement of the frontier Jívaro in the Ecuadorian socio-economic structure. The frontier Jívaro, primarily through their employment by Ecuadorians in manual labor, had acquired quantities of factory-manufactured goods. At the same time, there was a shortage of native-type goods among the Jívaro on the frontier, partially because of the near exhaustion of local game, which supplied feathers and bird skins for ornament. The interior Jívaro, in contrast, had a much more abundant supply of game and native-produced goods, but a greater scarcity of steel cutting tools and firearms. These complementary inequalities in supply and demand between the frontier and interior Jívaro formed the basis for the trade that supplied the latter with European-type technological items. Such technological items constituted almost the sole aspects of Western civilization that had been adopted by the interior Jívaro in 1956–57.

Chapter II

SHELTER, SUBSISTENCE, AND TECHNOLOGY

I am like an anaconda.
No one can get near my house
Because there is a lake around it.
I am a jaguar,
The bravest that is,
And no one
Can get near my house.

Sung by a man to his enemies
when he believes that they are
about to attack

The center of Jívaro life is the individual house, normally occupied by a polygynous nuclear family and surrounded by a garden in deep isolation in the forest. The house is typically built beside a small stream on a hillock where there are stands of soft or medium-hard wood. Such trees, especially palms, are easy to cut down to make garden clearings and are also preferred for house construction and firewood. The location of the house on high ground is not only better for drainage, but also furnishes a view across the surrounding garden to facilitate defensive fire in case of enemy attack (see Plate 2).

The dwelling is usually a large and well-made structure, oval in ground plan, with a single-gabled roof (see Figure 1). The roof is made of closely woven *kampanakä* palm thatch and is supported by nine center posts as well as by the smaller house wall posts. The windowless wall is built of stout chonta palm (*Guilielma* sp.) staves set vertically into the ground about an inch apart to permit light and air to enter,

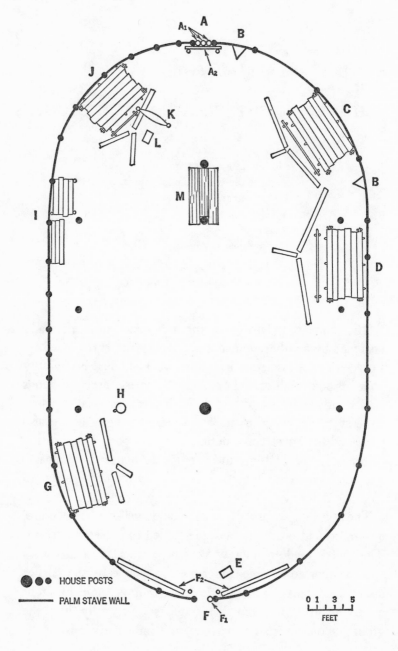

FIGURE I

Floor plan of a representative house (upper Río Cangaimi, 1957)

KEY TO FIGURE I

A   Doorway at women's end of the house

   A_1 Removable door posts in upright position

   A_2 Crossbar holding door posts in place

B   Chicken nest formed by a wedge of two palm slats against the base of the house wall

C   Older wife's palm-slat bed, with crossbar footrest and three fire logs

D   Married daughter's (and son-in-law's) bed

E   Ordinary rectangular stool (*kutaŋä*), placed for use by a male visitor

F   Doorway at men's end of the house

   F_1 Removable door post (left upright in the door)

   F_2 Removable door posts laid on the floor for use as visitors' benches

G   House owner's bed, for his daytime napping and for use by overnight visitors

H   House owner's round stool (*čimpuí*)

I   Palm-slat platforms built above the reach of small children for the storage of large pottery vessels

J   Younger wife's bed

K   Younger wife's baby's hammock, made of a piece of cloth suspended between two poles

L   Ordinary rectangular stool placed for use by the younger wife in cooking and making manioc beer

M   Split guadua bamboo platform suspended between house-posts to support food and beer bowls. Underneath are the large beer-brewing jars of both wives.

and to allow the inhabitants to see out and to fire at attackers. The interior of the dwelling is unpartitioned, constituting a single, long dirt-floored room with a doorway at each end. Floor plan dimensions of several houses were found to range from approximately 25 to 36 feet in width to about 40 to 60 feet in length. A representative house was 27 feet wide by 44 feet long with a maximum roof height of about 15 feet and with walls 7 feet high.

To protect the inhabitants from enemy attacks, the doorways (Figure 1, A, F) are closed with strong hand-hewn wooden doors or removable wooden posts locked into position with a crossbar. An extra layer of chonta palm staves is sometimes lashed to the house wall near the beds. This double wall covers the slits between the palm staves to protect sleeping members of the household from being shot by would-be nighttime assassins. If local feuding is at a particularly high pitch, logs may be laid horizontally against the inside of the house wall to form a breastwork about four feet high. Foxholes are also sometimes dug into the floor to permit firing from low points on the breastwork and to provide shelter for the women and children. A secret escape tunnel occasionally extends underneath the wall, coming up in the garden outside.

Houses ordinarily are occupied five to nine years, even though the gardens are abandoned more frequently, usually after three or four years' use. The chief reason given for abandoning the house after only five or six years is a scarcity of palm fire logs in the immediate vicinity. A dearth of wild game is often a supporting reason for early abandonment. If, however, palm logs and game remain plentiful, the dwelling is normally occupied until it starts rotting. The bases of the wall staves are usually the first parts to decay, but the house often is not abandoned until the roof begins to leak. Occasionally, such leakage does not occur significantly until the ninth year of occupancy.

If structural decay alone forces abandonment of a house, the new one is constructed sometimes only fifty to a hundred yards away. More frequently, however, poor hunting conditions necessitate the construction of the new structure two or three miles distant. Sometimes the scarcity of game requires a move to a greater distance, ten miles or more. In the not infrequent cases when a man and his family flee the neighborhood to escape assassination attempts, the new dwelling may be erected forty to eighty miles from the previous site. The death of the male head of the household is also cause for abandonment.

Houses are constructed by the men. While most of the building work technically could be done by the dwelling owner himself, he is generally helped by one or two close male relatives living nearby. The transportation and erection of the main house posts are the only tasks requiring a larger crew. For this effort, the owner invites about half a dozen male neighbors to help him.

Posts, beams, roof and walls are all lashed firmly together with strips of inner tree bark. Proceeding painstakingly, a man usually constructs a large and impressive structure capable of withstanding not only the natural elements and enemy attack, but also critical evaluation by his neighbors. The size and quality of a man's house is regarded as a serious indication of his personal "power," *kakarma*.

A family averaging only about nine persons typically occupies these rather large houses. While to a casual observer the size of the house might seem excessive in terms of everyday needs, the large floor space is deemed essential for hosting visitors, who are often guests coming to drink and dance. Since dancing is never done outdoors, where persons would be unprotected from rain and possible attackers, a large floor area is essential. A large house also makes it possible for neighboring relatives to congregate in the dwelling to make a combined stand against an expected enemy attack. Space needs are, in addition, particularly great when a *tsantsa* feast is given, since large numbers of guests dance and sleep within the house on such occasions. Under such circumstances, extra beds are built to line the walls.

The Jívaro divide the house conceptually and functionally into two halves: the men's end (*taɲamašä*), and the women's (*ekenta*). The men's half serves as a parlor and sleeping place for visitors. A couple of stools and a log door post or two serving as a bench are usually found in this end for the host and his visitors (Figure 1, H, E, F₂). The house owner's personal palm or bamboo slat bed is also located in the men's end (Figure 1, G) and, when there are visitors, is slept on by those male guests unaccompanied by wives. Sometimes, if there is not enough bed space, visitors will sleep on banana leaves spread on the dirt floor in the men's end of the house.

When there are no guests, the house owner uses the bed for his daytime napping, and for nighttime sleeping alone when his wife is menstruating or angry with him. Otherwise he sleeps with his wife on her bed in the women's half of the house. If he has more than one wife, there is a bed for each (Figure 1, J, C). Often an extra bed or two is also installed on the women's side for married couples who are visiting, or for a daughter and her husband during the period of temporary matrilocal residence within the house (Figure 1, D). Such beds are also utilized by who no longer sleep on their mother's bed. Split bamboo (*Guadua* sp.) shelves are suspended in the women's end between the center posts (Figure 1, M) and palm slat or split bamboo shelves (Figure 1, I) along the walls. These are used to store pottery and baskets of peanuts above the reach of small children. Occasionally a large wooden signal drum may be found leaning against a wall post. There are no other important permanent furnishings. The spaciousness of the house is matched by its neatness and cleanliness. The women sweep both inside and outside daily with a short broom made by lashing together branches of the *hapimiuk* plant. The sweepings are put on a banana leaf and carried away in an old basket to be dumped in the forest.

Smoldering fires are maintained at the foot of all beds both in the men's and women's ends to heat the sleepers' feet especially during the nights, which are often chilly, depending upon the altitude and the weather. Those at the women's beds are also the household cooking fires (see Plate 10). All household fires are made by laying three thick palm logs so that their ends meet like the spokes of a wheel. Normally, the log ends smolder slowly, but when a pot is set upon their juncture the logs soon burst into flame. With such an arrangement, fire lighting and kindling is rarely necessary. At night, additional light is provided by burning a small torch or two of copal.

Subsistence

Each household has either a single large garden or several smaller ones. In the latter case, the house itself is usually located in the largest. Such gardens constitute almost the exclusive source of carbohydrates for the Jívaro, providing, in terms of calories, perhaps about 65 per cent of the diet. The cultivation of slowly maturing tuberous plants, especially sweet manioc (*Manihot utilissima*), which can be harvested over long periods of time, the absence of a distinct dry season,[1] and a diversified crop inventory all contribute to making a continual supply of agricultural products possible throughout the year.

Crops grown for their tubers or corms include, besides sweet manioc, two varieties of sweet potato, *papa china* (from Spanish) [taro?], and three other members of the Araceae family (*saŋu, tuka, wančup*), the carrot-like *maya* (arracacha?), and peanuts. Of these, manioc is grown in by far the largest quantity, and is the chief source of starch. The most important non-tuberous food plants are plantains and "white" maize. Other crops grown in relatively small quantities are squash, red peppers, tomatoes, onions, the "gold" banana (*guineo de oro* in Spanish), pineapple, papaya, sugar cane, tobacco, achiote, gourds, cotton. *Tsapaŋ* (for heavy cordage), various fish poisons, medicinal plants, and hallucinogenic drugs, especially *Banisteriopsis* species and *Datura arborea*, are both cultivated in the garden and collected wild in the forest.

Gardens are abandoned after three plantings of manioc, in other words, after about three to five years, because of the growing amount of labor required to clear the ever increasing numbers of weeds. New garden clearings are made nearby in virgin timber except when the actual household is being moved, in which case the gardens are planted at the new house location. This practice of shifting gardens, the so-called "slash-and-burn" or swidden technique, is made possible by the plentiful supply of land. The Jívaro recognize this method, despite the necessity of making new clearings, as involving less effort than attempting to cope with the weeds at the old site.

If a man clears the forest without the aid of neighbors, he tends to make small clearings at different times, while the rarer communal effort results in one large clearing. Whether the garden area is in a single clearing or several, its total size is heavily influenced by the number of wives a man has to cultivate the fields. A household with one wife tends to have a garden of about 50,000 square feet, while a second spouse increases the area to about 65,000, and a third to approximately 75,000. The areal increases are usually not simple multiples of the number of wives because the demand for food and beer to feed visitors tends to lag behind the increments in additional wives. These figures vary, of course, according to the consumption demands of the household, its number of visitors, and the industry of its inhabitants. A man who wishes to gain prestige may clear garden areas of larger size for each of his wives. In such a case, a household in which there are two wives may sometimes have a total garden of 100,000 square feet or more.

By measuring the yield within a restricted section of garden, the writer was able to arrive at a rough estimate of the quantity of a single harvest per 10,000 square feet of cultivated land. The results indicate that a "one wife" household with a garden of some 50,000 square feet may yield these approximate amounts of the major crops: 300 bushels of manioc; a total of 180 bushels of *papa china*, Araceae corms and sweet potato combined; 300 pounds of peanuts; and 90 stems of plantains and bananas.

The preparation of a garden begins with clearing the forest. The head of the household, sometimes assisted by a son or son-in-law, fells and trims the trees and clears the undergrowth with a steel axe and machete. His wife (wives) and daughters (if any) drag the slashings into piles, which are burned ten to fourteen days later, provided the weather is sufficiently dry. Women do not assist in making clearings for maize, since the slashings, in the case of that crop, are left unburned on the ground where they fall. Occasionally a man may invite his neighbors to help him make a clearing, but this practice is infrequent.

All the above crops, except maize, are planted together in the same cleared plot. Manioc plants, which are the largest in the garden, are spaced slightly less than two yards apart throughout, with the smaller plants between them. A line of plantain and banana trees separates the garden from the forest.

Crop planting is done with two aboriginal tools and the machete. The former are a sharp-pointed planting stick thrust into the soil to make seed holes, and a flat-bladed palm wood digging stick used as a lever to excavate holes for planting and digging up manioc and other tubers and corms. The machete also functions as an excavating tool in planting.

Times of planting and harvesting overlap and thereby assure a constant reaping of agricultural staples. Sweet potato, *papa china*, and Araceae species are planted at any time of the year. Sweet potato and *papa china* mature in about six months, while the Araceae tubers and the carrot-like *maya* require a year. Plantain and banana are planted during a full moon at any time of the year, and are harvested twelve to fifteen months later. "White" maize and peanuts are usually sown semiannually at the blooming of the *šutsí* flower, maize maturing in seven months, the other crop in five.

The most important crop, sweet manioc, is planted and harvested daily in the same act. As the women dig up the manioc tubers, they place several cuttings from the same plant's stalk in the old hole and partially cover them with earth. Manioc matures in ten to twelve months, but the actual harvesting can, if desired, be delayed as much as an additional year. This continual replanting of the manioc crop on a year-round basis, as the individual plants are dug up, is an important factor in the reliability of Jívaro crop production. Thus the Jívaro, in a real sense, "store" much of their food in a living state in the ground and only need to dig it up, as desired, to supply food and to make the large quantities of manioc beer which constitute a basic part of their diet.

The manioc beer (*nihamanči*) is prepared by first peeling and washing the tubers in the stream near the garden. Then the water and manioc are brought to the house, where the tubers are cut up and placed in a pot to boil (see Plates 4, 5 and 10). When the manioc has become soft, the pot is removed from the fire and allowed to cool. The manioc is then mashed and stirred to a soft consistency with the aid of a special wooden paddle (see Plate 6). While the woman stirs the mash, she chews handfuls and spits them back into the pot, a process which may take half an hour or longer. The mastication of the mash is considered by the Jívaro to be essential to the proper and rapid fermentation of the brew, and their view seems to be supported by Western physicians who have informally voiced the opinion that the enzymes in the saliva, as well as the bacteria in the mouth, probably hasten the fermentation process.

After the mash has been prepared, it is transferred to a beer storage jar and left to ferment. Although the fermentation takes place rapidly, the beer is usually too much in demand to be allowed to sit very long. In being served, the beer is strained through a tree-gourd sieve to remove manioc fibers, and about one part of water is added to two parts of beer. The resultant liquid tastes somewhat like a pleasingly alcoholic buttermilk and is most refreshing. The Jívaro consider it to be far superior to plain water, which they drink only in emergencies such as when their beer canteens run dry while they are out hunting. Male informants, in addition, expressed the opinion that the beer is at its best if it has been chewed by a pretty girl rather than by an old woman. Beer is also made, in a slightly different fashion (see Plate 7), seasonally from the fruits of the chonta palm (*Guilielma utilis*).

A rough estimate of the average daily beer consumption of the adult male is three to four gallons; of the adult female, approximately one to two gallons; and of nine- to ten-year-old children, about half a gallon. The beer must ferment for four or five days to reach its maximum alcoholic content, but this is usually intentionally done only for feasts planned in advance. On the other hand, a jar or two of beer may reach such strength simply because it has not been consumed, in which case its availability provides an occasion to invite neighbors to come by for a drinking and dancing party.

The division of labor between men and women in agricultural activities is well defined. Women do most of the laborious garden work, being exlusively responsible for planting and harvesting manioc, Araceae species, sweet potato, *papa china*, red pepper, sugar cane, onion, and pineapple. Men and women work together to plant peanuts, but only women harvest them. Men alone plant and harvest maize. They also plant plantain and the "gold" bananas, but let the women do the harvesting. Women have sole responsibility for the arduous and never ending task of weeding. They use the machete as the weeding tool, scraping the earth to cut off all weeds at ground level. This task consumes the greatest amount of their time in the garden.

An idea of the nature of the sexual division of labor and, incidentally, of the importance of manioc beer, may be provided by the following log of a daily subsistence routine.

The husband gets up from his wife's bed at about 2 A.M., goes to the men's end of the house and sits down on a stool. He washes his mouth out with water from a gourd "bottle" at his side. He calls to his wife to "bring beer." She heats up some water and mixes it with manioc beer, and brings a pot of it to him. She serves him and an overnight male visitor by the light of a burning copal torch. Then she returns to her end of the house and boils plantains and manioc. She then gives each person a serving bowl of this food. Her husband, meanwhile, has been spinning cotton yarn and talking quietly with the male visitor. The wife brings more beer and serves it.

She goes back to her end of the house and remains seated and resting by the fire for about half an hour. Then she returns, bringing more beer. Since the men do not immediately finish the beer, she stays crouching by the side of her husband, listening to the conversation (she has just eaten a little bit of manioc herself in the women's end of the house). She returns there, remains approximately half an hour, and then brings beer again. She goes back to her end of the house again for about another half hour, and then returns with more beer. This time she stays to chat a bit with her husband and then goes back to her area. It is now almost dawn.

The husband calls out to his wife to bring beer. She carries in a large pot of beer and serves continually from it until dawn. He then informs her that he is going hunting, and puts beer in his calabash canteen, takes some boiled manioc in a net bag, and his gun, and sets off with his wife and hunting dogs. The children stay at home.

They return home from the hunt at about 2 P.M., having killed an agouti. As soon as they arrive, the man asks his wife to bring him beer, which she does. Then he butchers the agouti and she boils it in a pot. When it is cooked, she brings the pot to the middle of the house and takes out all the meat, placing it on fresh banana leaves. She calls the men to come and eat. They arise, picking up their stools, and move to the banana leaves. Then all the children come and squat around them. The wife gives one piece of meat to each child, and a separate serving bowl of meat to the male visitor.

When all is eaten, the men get up and return with their stools to where they were sitting before. They rinse their mouths and hands with water from the gourd "bottle." Then the husband, getting up, calls to his wife to bring beer. Having drunk more beer, he lies down on the bed in the men's end of the house. He rests until approximately 5 P.M., while his wife goes to the garden, brings back manioc, and cooks it. He then gets up and tells his wife to bring beer. She carries in calabash bowls of beer. The husband then tells her to bring manioc and meat.

After this meal, his wife brings in a small pot of beer. The men take only two servings of beer apiece, and then converse. They talk about twenty minutes, and take new servings of beer. The wife stays at the side of her husband during these twenty minutes, sometimes participating in the conversation. After this second serving, the wife returns to her end of the house, and the men continue talking until dark. Then the wife brings in a copal torch and lights it. They talk once more and then drink beer again. Finally they finish the pot of beer and the wife returns to her end of the house with it. There she goes to bed, while the men continue their conversation. She rests about half an hour, when her husband calls her to serve beer. She brings a pot of it. The men drink and she remains with them. When they finish the beer, the wife returns to her end of the house, washes out the pot and the calabash serving bowl, and stores them for the night. Then she goes to bed. After half an hour, the men go to bed also, her husband joining her in the women's end of the house, the male visitor sleeping on the husband's daytime bed in the men's end of the house.

For the same household, this is a record of an alternative schedule, on a day when the husband decided to fell trees to make a garden clearing instead of going hunting. The routine up to dawn is similar:

Then he tells his wife of his intention to work clearing trees. She puts a pot of beer into a carrying basket and packs manioc and plantains around it. She supports the basket with a tumpline over the forehead, carries an empty cooking pot in her right hand, a firebrand in her left hand, and the axe under her arm. Leaving the children in the house, she sets forth down the trail with her husband, who carries only his gun and his machete.

When they arrive at the spot where trees are to be felled, she fetches wood, makes a fire, and cooks manioc. Her husband starts felling trees. After about two hours he calls for beer. He drinks two or three gourd bowls full and continues working. In about another hour he calls for beer again and drinks a similar amount. He tells his wife to cook meat and continues working. Around noon he goes to where she has been cooking, and asks for beer, drinking three gourd bowls full. She serves boiled meat, putting it, with boiled manioc and roasted plantains, on fresh banana leaves. When they finish eating, he drinks beer again, and returns to his work. He fells trees for about an hour, comes back and drinks more beer.

Then they return home. When they arrive, he sits down on his stool and asks for beer. At about 2 P.M., his daughter and son-in-law, who live a few hundred yards away, drop by and join in drinking beer. They all begin to social-dance and, since there is ample beer brewed, they continue drinking and dancing all afternoon and late into the night. They drink beer continually and do not bother to prepare or eat any food. The children drink beer, too, and munch on cold boiled manioc. By about 3 A.M., everyone has fallen asleep, the daughter and son-in-law staying overnight in the house. They all sleep until early the next afternoon, when they eat.

Hunting is the chief source of protein, and is more important to the food supply than fishing or gathering, contributing an estimated 20 per cent of the diet. A great diversity of botanical and zoological species exists in this region,[2] but this variety is typically accompanied by low density of population for any particular species. This low density sometimes poses a problem for Indians engaged in collecting a specific kind of wild fruit or hunting a particular species of game. This situation is aggravated for the hunter by the fact that virtually all of the Jívaro territory has been hunted efficiently for a long period of time, with the result that game is not as abundant as in regions unoccupied by the Indians. This fact was particularly driven home to my Jívaro companions and me in 1969, when, in traveling through an unhunted "no-man's-land" between the Jívaro and the Achuara along the lower Río Cangaimi, which had not been exploited because of the enmity between the two groups, we encountered unprecedented quantities of monkeys and birds.

The Jívaro, under the circumstances, do not normally find collecting a very rewarding activity, and, in hunting, they cannot afford the luxury of specializing in a few large game animals, such as might be possible in some other environments. The blowgun, suitable for hunting game ranging from small birds to large monkeys, therefore, becomes a very important food-securing weapon.

Mammals especially important to subsistence include peccary, agouti, and such monkeys as howler, squirrel, capuchin, and black. Peccary and monkey are valued for both their skins and flesh, while the agouti and armadillo are utilized generally for the meat alone. Most species of birds, except for carrion-eaters, are hunted almost daily as sources of food and for their plumage. Birds most often killed include species of parrot, toucan, dove, and curassow. Both the large and small species of toucan are particularly prized for their pelts and feathers; jaguar, ocelot and other feline species are commonly hunted for their skins (see Plate 9). Rabbits and deer, although present, are never hunted for food, the former because they are "like rats," the latter for supernatural reasons (see p. 150).

Stalking is the chief hunting technique, both for arboreal and ground-dwelling creatures. Monkeys and large birds are usually stalked with the blowgun (see Plate 8) and darts poisoned with curare (unpoisoned darts suffice for small birds). A poisoned dart is notched around its tip so that it will break off if a monkey tries to remove it. The hunter, usually alone, but sometimes with a male companion, waits until the monkeys are calling among themselves before stepping stealthily to the base of the monkeys' tree and blowing. The maximum effective range of the blowgun rarely exceeds 100 feet, but the silence of the weapon often permits the hunter to shoot several individuals before the troop becomes alarmed and swings off through the trees. The shot monkeys drop from the trees within a few minutes. The blowgun is not considered satisfactory for hunting ground-dwelling creatures, which are killed instead with shotguns and old Winchester .44 carbines, loaded either with shot or, rarely, in the case of the latter weapon, with bullets. Shy birds, such as the toucan, are hunted more with firearms than with the shorter-range blowgun.

The blowguns and curare dart poison are obtained almost entirely by trade from the Achuara, the Jívaro acknowledging themselves to be inferior blowgun makers and stating that they do not possess the right plants in their region to produce first-rate poison. The blowguns themselves are about seven feet long and made of a single piece of chonta palm which has been split down its length into two pieces which are grooved with great precision and bound together with fiber strips cemented into place with a black beeswax coating.

Blowgun darts are easily made, in a fraction of a minute, by whittling the slender ribs of ivory nut palm leaves. In hunting, the darts are carried in a quiver around the neck or stuck through the hair over the ear, wrapped at one end with kapok to provide resistance when blown. The speed with which the darts are produced makes the blowgun an extremely economical weapon to operate compared, for example, to the bow and arrow, with which the Jívaro are not acquainted. Arrow making, as I have observed among the Conibo Indians of the Río Ucayali region of eastern Peru, is a comparatively time-consuming process, and there is always the danger of losing arrows in the treetops when hunting monkeys or birds. Blowgun darts, on the other hand, are so easy to make that their loss means little to the hunter. Also, from what I have observed, blowguns tend to be more accurate in hunting small birds at close range. A final hunting advantage, compared to the bow and arrow, is that the motion involved in using the weapon is so slight, and the flight of the darts so unnoticeable, that game is rarely disturbed if the hunter misses his target. Of course, compared to a firearm, the blowgun is even more economical, but limited in range and not sufficiently fast-acting on large or dangerous game.

Dogs are commonly used in hunting peccary, jaguars, and ocelots, although a hunter, armed with a shotgun or carbine, may stalk them alone. When taking a dog on a peccary hunt, the man is accompanied by a wife, who handles the leashed dog, and also is frequently assisted by another male hunter. Even in hunting dangerous felines, only one dog is used to tree the cat, but up to a dozen people may participate.

Blinds, game calls, and traps are the main supplementary hunting devices. Conical blinds, made by sticking palm fronds into the ground, may be constructed at feeding places of toucans, agouti, or other creatures. Game calls are employed both in blinds and when stalking. Hunters call parrots without the aid of any devices, but blow against the edge of a leaf held between cupped hands to summon toucans. An ingeniously carved vegetable ivory mouthpiece is used to call agouti. This device often brings agouti to within fifteen to thirty feet of the hunter. Agouti are also sometimes dug out of their burrows by the hunters with digging sticks and aided by hunting dogs. If such efforts fail, traps are set at the mouths of the holes. Traps are otherwise rarely used.

The characteristic hunting expedition is undertaken by the individual hunter, with or without a wife and dogs, and does not usually extend beyond about eight miles from the house. He leaves the house at dawn and, if successful in killing a large animal such as monkey, peccary, or agouti, usually is home by early afternoon. If, however, the hunting is becoming poor in his area, and he has failed to secure meat for several days, he may range so far that he does not return home until dusk. He continues to go out every day until he succeeds in his quest.

When a man kills a large animal, he normally does not go hunting again for four or five days. A typical routine is as follows: the first day after returning from a successful hunt, he fells trees and clears slash for a garden; the next two days he rests, and does spinning and weaving in the house; the fourth day he goes to visit friendly relatives; and the fifth day he goes hunting again.

A second kind of hunting expedition takes place every two months or so in which the hunter, accompanied by a wife and also often by another friendly couple or two, spends about five days in more remote parts of the forest, usually seeking monkeys. Troops of monkeys are more efficiently hunted by men working together, since one hunter alone can usually only kill a fraction of the troop before the rest are startled and flee. The expedition is usually continued until its supply of manioc, plantains, and manioc beer is about to run out.

To assure success in hunting, young men (both married and unmarried) may join together in a small group under the supervision of an older master of ceremony (*wea*) to inhale tobacco smoke for a three-day period during which they alternate the smoke-inhalation sessions with hunting in the forest with blowguns. During the ritual sessions, called *kusupan*, the men take turns blowing tobacco smoke through guadua bamboo tubes into each other's lungs. It is believed that a man must entirely swallow the smoke he receives in order to be certain that he will not fail as a hunter.

A variety of fish and shellfish is present in streams and rivers, but swift currents and the small size of many watercourses seem to limit the degree of emphasis on their exploitation in many localities. Fishing roughly contributes perhaps only a little over 5 per cent of the total diet, significantly less than hunting. Corvina, suckers, and sheat-fish are taken from main streams and rivers, while crayfish and fresh-water crabs are gathered in the shallows.

Fishing techniques range from simply seizing fish by hand to complex river-poisoning operations. The fish that are caught bare-handed belong mostly to a species (*nayumpï*) capable of fastening itself to the underside of river boulders by means of a suction pad appendage. Hook-and-line fishing is done from a riverbank. Any handy stick is used for a pole, while an iron trade hook is baited with a piece of manioc, ripe plantain, or an earthworm.

A few men possess rectangular throw nets for catching medium-sized fish. A pair of fishermen, or a man and his wife, enter the shallows about ten feet apart. One tosses an end of the net to his companion with a circular motion. As the net is drawn to shore, balsa wood floats support its top edge, while stone sinkers keep it vertical in the water. Good-sized fish are also caught in deeper waters with a special thin, long palm wood thrusting spear.

Fish poisoning is undertaken perhaps every few weeks to secure a large catch. Men, women, and children from several neighboring houses usually participate. They select a section of river where it is bisected by an island or sandbar, to which the men and boys construct a low dam of river boulders from one bank. This stone dam is constructed to form a lagoon where the poison can sufficiently take effect in the slowed current. Other men meanwhile build split bamboo grating-like fish traps at several low points on the dam and prepare the fish poison.

Three types of plant piscicides are used: *timu* (in Spanish, *barbasco*), *masu*, and *payaš*. *Timu* is considered the best of these, but is used in combination with *masu* for maximum success. Large quantities are required, and the fishermen often prepare six to eight bushel-sized baskets. They pound the plants to a pulp between river boulders and dump them into the water upstream. If all goes well, within twenty to thirty minutes stunned fish begin rising to the surface and float toward the dam. The men who constructed the traps seize the fish as they are washed onto the bamboo gratings. Everyone else, regardless of age or sex, wades into the lagoon and grabs for fish. Each person owns whatever he catches, although he often may give some of his catch to a less fortunate participant. Fish poisoning is sometimes pursued at night because the fish tend to be nearer the surface and therefore more susceptible to the poison. Both poisoning and netting are most effectively conducted during dry periods, when the rivers and streams are low and the current slow.

Gathering activities contribute quantitatively relatively little to the diet, approximately 5 per cent annually, but do provide a variety of delicacies to supplement it. Various species of insects and fruits, shoots and leaves constitute the main kinds of gathered foods.

Insects particularly are relished as food items, both in larval and mature forms. The rotten cores of fallen chonta palms are cut open to collect cocoons of two kinds of edible grubs (*mukintü, čarančam*), and the ivory nut palm often yields larvae of a large moth (*wampaŋ*). Cocoons containing grubs of the butterfly *tampiruša* are removed from hanging vines. Leaf-eating ants (*aiyaŋü*) and a kind of grasshopper (*tsampuntä*) also are collected.

The various species of palms are the most important source of wild plant food. The chonta (*Guilielma utilis*), royal, and other palms (*kiŋak, kuakaš, ampakai, tirintä*) are chopped down with machetes to obtain their edible tips. Except for the *ampakai*, these palms (together with the ivory nut palm and *kumai*) also supply an annual harvest of large clusters of edible fruits, which are both eaten boiled and made into beer. Frequently young tender leaves are collected from other plants (*uŋusï, tučinč, ipü, waŋat*), but no wild roots are dug up for food. Generally, the only tool used in all these gathering activities is the machete.

Virtually all families raise chickens, some also raise ducks, and a very few keep pigs. A household's pigs are allowed to wander relatively freely in the adjacent forest to feed. If they start rooting in the garden, a low rail fence may be built around it to keep them out. Neighbors' pigs never seem to threaten the garden, because of the long distances between houses and the small numbers of pigs kept.

Chickens, ducks, and their eggs are utilized for food, especially to feed visitors when no game is on hand. In the uncommon cases where pigs are kept, the family usually is planning a *tsantsa* feast and intends to slaughter the pigs to feed the large number of anticipated guests, who could not be supplied with enough meat from hunting alone. Normally, however, the contribution of the animal domesticates, essentially fowl, is less than 5 per cent of the diet.

At least one or two dogs are kept in most households. These not only aid in hunting in the forest, as mentioned earlier, but also protect the garden crops, including the manioc tubers, from devastation by agouti and other rodents. A family without a good hunting dog lives in fear of losing much of its garden produce within a few months. An equally important service that they provide is to act as watchdogs against surprise attacks. Leashed to beds in the women's end of the house (see Plate 11), their slightest barking usually results in the household head seizing his gun and preparing to defend himself and his family. Since the dogs' barking indicates that the intended victim has been alerted, the attacking party generally withdraws. Interestingly, the name for dog, *niawá*, is the same term used to designate the feared and respected jaguar.

The importance of dogs in hunting, protecting the garden, and defense helps to explain the high degree of care they receive. When puppies are born, one of the owner's wives observes a kind of couvade, in which she lies abed with the bitch to protect the litter from supernatural harm. A puppy is nursed by the wife as well as by its canine mother. Even in adult life, the dog normally sleeps on the bed beside its owners, and is fed premasticated manioc in a special wooden dish. Dogs, like people, are even given the hallucinogenic *Datura* to help them obtain supernatural power.

The majority of households contain at least one pet besides the dog. Such pets, which include monkeys, marmosets, parakeets, parrots, macaws, and doves, are captured and tamed, both for personal amusement and for trade to the western or frontier Jívaro to obtain steel machetes, axe-heads, firearms, and ammunition.

Technology and Crafts

No single tool can be considered more ubiquitous in Jívaro life than the machete. The machete is the sole garden weeding implement as well as the only tool used for digging up root crops including the staple food, sweet manioc. It is used for woodworking, to dig clay for pottery, to prepare foods and to cut hair, and it is used to fell even the largest tree, although the less common steel axe is preferred for this task when it is available.

Machetes are of two types: the more plentiful *hapa mačit* ("deer machete"), of Ecuadorian manufacture, which was formerly obtained at Macas in exchange for one deer carcass; and the *kayens mačit* (Collins machete), of North American manufacture and preferred by the Jívaro because of its superior efficiency. The *hapa mačit* was introduced first, the Collins implement not reaching the Jívaro until about 1941. During the past few decades, large single-bitted steel axe heads have also been introduced in significant numbers by means of a system of Jívaro trading partners. Such axes are still far less plentiful than machetes, but in great demand because of their superiority over machetes in felling trees. Iron adze blades, which were apparently introduced about the same time as machetes, are possessed by only a very few individuals, but are in demand for finishing canoes and stools. All the types of steel tools are mainly obtained by trade from the western or frontier Jívaro of the Río Upano Valley.

As machetes become worn through years of continual use

and lose their handles, they are relegated to purely culinary tasks. The steel blades are so highly valued, however, that they continue to be used even when worn down to mere stubs. Such stubs are broken into small triangular pieces and then used as knives for whittling blowgun darts and for performing other small cutting jobs. Wooden objects made with the machete are characteristically simple but well made, although a few carved embellishments resembling reptile heads may be seen as the handles of stools and mortar boards, and as the tips of house posts and the prows of dugout canoes.

The machete is the basic tool used in manufacturing objects from bone and the shells of large land snails, the latter material being utilized primarily for women's dance belt rattles. Bone work is limited to making needles from monkey leg bones and carving gunpowder containers of cows' horns traded from the frontier Jívaro.

Non-ferrous cutting tools are nowadays only rarely employed. A sharp-edged strip of bamboo is used to cut the umbilicus of a new-born infant; and sometimes a hardwood weed-cutting "machete" is used in garden work when there is no steel one available. Otherwise steel tools dominate the processing of materials.

The tip of a machete or machete fragment serves as a boring tool, awls being unknown. Men sew the fringes of garments and make knotless netting bags with the aid of monkey bone needles. A few possess large steel needles for the same purposes. Women use bone or steel needles, or a fragment of a blowgun dart, to pin their dresses (*taráči*) over one shoulder (see Plate 4).

Wooden mortar boards and pestles are utilized in mashing the fruit of the chonta palm to prepare a special beer, to mash peanuts, and to crush a mixture of salt and hot pepper (see Plate 7). The same wooden board is used with a crude rocker-stone to crush maize for chick feed. The wooden planting and digging sticks used in agricultural work have been mentioned previously.

Vessels are made by the women from clay and gourds. All pottery is manufactured by the method of coil construction and vessels are finished by scraping. Three kinds of clay are used for different types of vessels. Carbonized bark of the *apáčaram* tree is powdered for tempering material in food bowls, while sand temper is used in drinking bowls, fermentation jars, and cooking jars. All vessels except cooking jars are coated with red achiote or black beeswax after firing. Only the interiors of large drinking bowls, the exteriors of miniature drinking bowls, and the interior necks of fermentation jars are ever decorated. Even then, such decoration is usually simple and hastily made, often consisting of unelaborated irregular zigzag and dot patterns in vegetal paint. The one apparent exception is the miniature drinking bowls, which sometimes have intricate and well-executed designs. These, however, are obtained by trade from the Canelos tribe to the north.

The fermentation jars are the largest vessels made, averaging about ten to thirteen gallons in capacity. These jars, covered with a drinking bowl or banana leaf, serve to store the fermenting manioc or chonta palm fruit beer. Next in size are the cooking jars, the largest of which are employed to boil the hallucinogenic *Banisteriopsis* for resident or visiting shamans. The other chief ceramic vessels are food-serving bowls and the two sizes of drinking bowls. Small pottery or gourd jars serve to store the curare blowgun dart poison. One special miniature pottery bowl is used by old men to brew an emetic tea from *Ilex* sp. leaves.

Large long-handled gourds hold water for cooking and

beer making, while shorter ones store the water with which the men rinse their mouths upon arising and after eating. Other gourds are cut in half and perforated to serve as sieves in straining manioc fibers out of the beer. Tree gourds are used by men as canteens for carrying the thick beer mash when hunting or traveling far.

Three kinds of baskets are made, all by the men: a plaited openwork basket used primarily for carrying and storing food; a wickerwork type for carrying fish; and a relatively insect-proof plaited and double-walled basket with a banana leaf lining and a cover for storing featherwork and other personal effects. Matting is unknown.

Virtually every adult male possesses at least one firearm for hunting and fighting. While there are a few ancient Winchester .44 carbines obtained from the Achuara, almost all the guns are Spanish-made muzzle-loading shotguns of recent manufacture secured primarily from trading partners dwelling in the region of white contact in the Río Upano Valley.

Most of the Winchester carbines, although originally pump-action weapons, are so worn that they can function only as single-shot weapons. For fighting, they are loaded with highly valued .44 pistol cartridges obtained through native trading partners from the Achuara, who in turn secure the cartridges from other trading partners in Peru. For hunting, the cartridges are simply reloaded with black powder and shot, and the cartridge primer is replaced with the type used on muzzle-loading shotguns.

The shotguns, percussion-cap weapons usually with a 20-gauge bore, are much preferred over the Winchesters for hunting and also are much more plentiful throughout the tribe due to their steady acquisition by means of the native trading partnerships. They are loaded with black powder

and iron shot of assorted sizes obtained from the frontier
Jívaro, or loaded with the hard seeds of the *etsa* tree, or
even river gravel, when iron shot cannot be obtained.

Fighting is rarely done with weapons other than firearms,
but occasionally a man kills an enemy from ambush with a
plain palm lance or a "shotgun" lance to demonstrate his
valor. The "shotgun" lance has a tip made by chopping off
the barrel of a worn-out shotgun with a machete, beating
the base of the barrel into a point, and inserting a palm-wood
shaft into the muzzle end of the barrel. A few old men also
carry lances with iron tips obtained years ago by trade from
Gualaquiza. Some of these older men also have crude wooden
shields in their houses for use in the *tsantsa* feast ritual. Machetes and the less common trade knives are also sometimes
employed as fighting weapons.

Men stretch and dry skins of wild boar, jaguar, ocelot, and
other felines for trade. Monkey hides are used for making
men's shoulder bags. Both sexes manufacture thread, string,
and braided rope. Thread is made from the inner bark of the
tsaké tree, and string from the inner bark of the *kumai* palm.
Men's shoulder bags of knotted and knotless netting are made
of this inner bark string using large bone needles.

Weaving, done in almost all houses, is exclusively a man's
task. Men, compared to women in Jívaro society, tend to have
much more leisure time, which may help account for the fact
that they do the spinning, dyeing, and weaving. When not
hunting or clearing forest, a man likes to sit in his end of the
house, either quietly alone or conversing with visitors. In
either case, spinning and weaving allow him to occupy his
hands with a pleasant craft which can be interrupted or
picked up again as he desires. The textiles he makes are extremely durable and thus there is usually no urgency attached

to the task. A man normally takes pride in his ability as
a weaver, as evidenced by this yarn-spinning song:

> For me it is very easy
> To spin yarn,
> For I am a man-spider.
> I am a man-spider.
> Therefore I am adept.
>
> My hand is like the hand
> Of a spider.
> Because of this
> I make the spindle hum.

Men spin yarn from home-grown cotton and dye it by
dipping it into vegetal solutions. Special clay is sometimes
rubbed into wet yarn to produce dark shades. European dyes
still are unknown. Cotton kilts (*itipï*) of a standard size and
decoration are woven on a backstrap loom. Women's dresses
(*taračï*) are made by sewing two such cotton kilts together.

The home-woven kilts and dresses are the most common
type of daily dress. Both men's kilts and women's dresses are
simply pieces of cloth wrapped around the body and held
together by a string or belt. The men's kilt is typically held
in place by a bark string, while the women's dress is fastened
over the right shoulder, and a string or home-woven cotton
belt keeps it closed. Both garments are made of heavily
woven cloth highly resistant to tearing, and capable of en-
during daily wear for about four years.

While home-woven garments constitute the daily garb, the
wearing of machine-woven trade clothing or cloth is reserved
for visiting and receiving visitors. At such times, men who
have trade shirts put them on, and men who possess two

home-woven kilts wear the newer of the pair. Less frequently, a man also possesses a pair of trousers for special wear (see Plate 16). A few women, who have obtained machine-manufactured cloth, make their own "party dresses." Sometimes a man has an Achuara-made kilt, which he saves for visiting.

Families lacking woven cloth make kilts and dresses from bark cloth. Such clothing is much inferior in durability, and is considered an indication of family indolence and weakness.

Nuŋuí

Agricultural subsistence, especially, is connected with a system of belief which surrounds an "earth mother" named Nuŋuí. Whether Nuŋuí is best viewed as a class of crop fairies or as a goddess appears to be a difficult matter to decide.[8] On the one hand, the Jívaro usually speak of Nuŋuí in the singular, but they deny that there is just one, saying that there are "many," although all are identical in their attributes. For convenience, Nuŋuí will be referred to here in the singular.

Nuŋuí, it is believed, is responsible for pushing the crops up through the ground, i.e., for their growth. Without her help, a woman cannot expect to be successful as a gardener and, therefore, engages in various practices to attract Nuŋuí to the garden, and to keep her there. Such practices are based upon a knowledge of Nuŋuí's two main demands from the Jívaro: to be given a place to dance and to be provided with "babies."

It is believed that Nuŋuí, who is about three feet high, very fat, and dressed in a black *tarači*, according to those who have seen her in dreams and hallucinogen-induced visions, likes to come out at night and dance in the gardens, which, of course, are the only unobstructed clearings in the forest. She is most attracted to brand-new gardens with a minimum of growth and, in fact, such open spaces are so attractive that many Nuŋuí may come to dance simultaneously in such a clearing. However, normally there is only one Nuŋuí associated with a single garden and she dances alone between the manioc plants, in turn dancing as a partner with each pair of the opening shoots of manioc. As long as the garden is well weeded, she will probably stay at the site, remaining underground during the day. Her continued presence assures that she will be pushing up the crops, including all the domesticated plants. If, however, the woman responsible for the garden fails to weed it adequately, Nuŋuí will withdraw deep into the ground and remove herself to some other woman's better-weeded plot, "taking" the crop with her, and also causing the weeds suddenly to become even worse in the garden she has left. For this reason the Jívaro say they must weed the gardens carefully. Indeed, those with the best-weeded gardens do tend to have the best crop production, which is given as evidence of the validity of their belief.

With the breaking of day, Nuŋuí returns underground, going deeper as the day progresses. Since her supernatural force retreats with her, it is believed that the manioc tubers and sweet potatoes diminish in size gradually during the daytime. For this reason, the mistress of the garden prefers to dig up the tuberous crops early in the morning, while they still retain their maximum size. At the same time, going early in the morning to the garden may frighten Nuŋuí, so the woman sings a song of propitiation to reassure Nuŋuí and to keep her from submerging more deeply. Sometimes the woman simply thinks the song without opening her mouth, for it is believed that Nuŋuí can hear it this way as well. A typical version is as follows:

> I am a woman of Nuŋuí.
> Therefore I sing,
> So that the manioc will grow well.
> For when I do not sing,
> There is not much production.
> I am of Nuŋuí.
> Therefore I harvest faster than others.

In addition to providing Nuŋuí with a dancing place and treating her with respect through songs, the mistress of the garden provides her with "babies" to encourage her to remain at the garden. These are three red stones which appear to the women in hallucinogen-induced visions and dreams as babies for Nuŋuí. The stones, which are chips of unworked red jasper, are known as the "stones of Nuŋuí" or the "stones of manioc" and supposedly can only be found through having a dream in which Nuŋuí appears and tells the woman, "I am hiding a 'stone of manioc' in such-and-such a place." Then the woman must go out early in the morning, before eating, to find the stone, because if she were to delay, it would disappear as Nuŋuí made her morning withdrawal down into the earth. Only one such stone is found as a result of a given dream, and each is jealously hoarded. They are hidden in the center of the garden under an overturned food-serving bowl. A myth explaining the origin of this practice is as follows:

In the olden time there was no manioc or any other agricultural crop. The people just ate the leaf of the *uŋusï* [a species of the Araceae]. In that time many people died of hunger. Since they were hungry, they said, "Let us go to this stream. Let us catch crabs." As they caught crabs, they followed the stream and encountered a woman washing off sweet potatoes, taro [?], manioc, and peanuts. This woman was Nuŋuí. There were many Nuŋuí there. The people asked that these Nuŋuí give them food because they lacked food and fire. One Nuŋuí had a fat little female baby. She said, "Take this little baby. It is of manioc." But she also said, "Don't beat my baby, or everything will disappear. And never leave her alone in the house, but always take her with you."

So the people took the baby, whose name was Čiki, back to their house. The woman of the family household told it, "Cause manioc to come here." So the baby said, "Let there be manioc." Immediately manioc filled the house. Then the woman said, "I desire a garden." The baby said, "Let there be a garden." At that moment a garden appeared with all kinds of food. Then the woman said, "Now I want a large beer brewing jar." Instantly there were many beer brewing jars. The woman then said, "I now want two of the brewing jars to be filled with beer." Immediately two of the jars were filled with manioc beer. "Now I want meat here." Then plenty of smoke-dried meat appeared. Then she said, "I want many fish." Instantly there were many fish.

These people always took the baby with them, as Nuŋuí had told them to do. As the baby grew bigger, the children of these people grew bigger also. So one day the women went to work in the garden and left the children to take care of the baby. One of the children said to the baby, "We would like to see snakes and boa constrictors." Immediately many snakes and boa constrictors arrived. Then they went away. Then a child said, "Now I want a demon [iwančí]." Immediately many demons came. Then one of the children said to the baby, "Why did you bring snakes and demons?", and threw ashes in the baby's eyes. The baby began to cry. Then the other child said, "Now I want a dried monkey complete with its head [monkey heads, including the brains, are considered to be a particular delicacy]. Then many monkeys and other animals appeared, but without heads.

Since all of these animals lacked heads, this child began to beat the baby, and the other child continued throwing ashes in the baby's eyes. The baby began calling for its Nuŋuí mother. It climbed up on top of the thatch roof and remained there crying and calling, "Come, mother, let us start eating the peanuts."

There was much guadua bamboo growing near the house, and at this moment the bamboo began waving as if there were a great wind, so that it almost touched the house. Finally the bamboo fell over onto the house and the baby grasped one of the trunks. Meanwhile the manioc in the garden started disappearing into the ground, and the women came rushing back to the house. By this time, the baby had entered a section of the bamboo and sat inside of it as though on a stool [the guadua bamboo often has a diameter of six inches or more]. The women asked what had happened, and the children told them. Immediately, a woman picked up a machete and started chopping up the bamboo to find the baby. She finally found the baby and told it to bring back lots of manioc. But all the baby said was "Čiki." And it only brought forth čiki [an emetic].

Nuŋuí said, "I told you not to beat the baby. Now that you have beaten the baby, you will have to suffer a great deal." The entire garden and the trails then disappeared into the ground. This is the reason that nowadays we put stones in the garden, for these red stones appear in the women's dreams as babies. Thus we are giving Nuŋuí babies.

Besides providing domesticated plant food both originally and on a daily basis, Nuŋuí also is said to have given the Jívaro their knowledge of successful pottery making. A version of the myth is as follows:

In the old time there were two orphans, a boy and a girl, who broke a pot. The woman who owned it beat them, and they went off, crying, into the forest. They finally came across a trail. But it was not really a trail; it just looked like one. On the trail they encountered Nuŋuí digging clay out of the ground. She told them, "I am Nuŋuí, and I give all the people their food. I shall teach you a song. Sing it, because you are orphans, and make pots. Take some of this clay, and as soon as you get home, make pots with it."

The children obeyed her and found themselves able to make all kinds of pots which did not break when they fired them. There had been pots before, but usually they broke in firing. The children told everyone about their success. When they grew up, their houses contained many pots, they had excellent gardens, and many people came to ask them for pots. The orphans' crops flourished, their chickens and pigs multiplied remarkably, more than those of anyone else, and they taught the other people the song which they use to this day to prevent the pots from cracking during firing.

Nuŋuí is also believed to have given the dog to the Jívaro for hunting. This association of dogs with Nuŋuí is consistent with the importance of the dogs in protecting the gardens from rodents and other destructive animals, and with the fact that they are cared for by the women. In fact, when a man wishes to hunt game that requires the assistance of a dog, he asks a wife to accompany him, and to handle the dog on a leash. It is believed that the presence of the woman, through her connection to Nuŋuí, will help the man have better luck, and she constantly (and usually silently) sings to Nuŋuí for success in getting game and also so that the dog will be protected from snakebite or other misfortune.

Women also sing to Nuŋuí to help protect the household from attack by enemies who might be approaching through the surrounding garden. That is, they believe that the manioc plants especially have an innate desire and capability to suck the blood from any person touching them. A woman, therefore, sings to them to suck the blood of enemies, but not of

members of the family. A portion of one such song is as
follows:

> Don't suck the blood of my husband
> And also don't suck the blood of my daughter.
> When you want to suck blood,
> Suck the blood of my enemies.
> When my husband comes,
> He will look very beautiful and very clear.
> But when our enemies come,
> They will come very pale
> And in the form of demons.[4]
> And you will know
> Who will die,
> Who will die.
> And when they enter this garden,
> They will have their blood sucked.
> All, all I can call,
> Even the plantain itself.
> I am a woman of Nuŋuí.

To protect themselves from such blood sucking, visitors
to other persons' houses sometimes stick a branch of manioc
in their belts in order to pass safely through a thick stand of
the plant. Parents also employ the blood-sucking belief in
telling children why they should not play in the garden.

Chapter III

SOCIAL RELATIONS

When I die
You will look for young men.
But while I live
Put more beer
In this beautiful bowl.
Let us dance, my little wife.

Social dance song

The interior Jívaro are scattered in some 245 houses over an estimated area of 1,844 square miles (4,775 square kilometers).[1] The territory maximally involved extends roughly from near the Río Chiguasa south-southeastward to the upper Río Yaupi and from the western slopes of the Cordillera de Cutucú eastward to the Río Pangui (see Map 2). With an estimated nine persons per house, the total number of Jívaro utilizing this area would be approximately 2,205, or 1.19 persons per square mile (.46 persons per square kilometer). Nowhere is this population concentrated into villages, being instead dispersed in loose-knit neighborhood groupings of irregular size. The interior Jívaro "community" is a neighborhood of widely distributed households in which membership is not formally or usually very clearly defined and in which the abundance of land is accompanied by an absence of definitions or claims of territoriality.

A person's definition of his neighborhood usually depends upon his distance from it. For example, if his home is near the *niawá entsa* (jaguar stream) tributary of the Río Cangaimi, and the speaker is at home or visiting the house of a Jívaro on another tributary of the Cangaimi, the visitor will use the name of his home tributary stream as the label for his group, e.g., *niawá šuarä* (people of the jaguar stream). If the same speaker is a day's journey away, however, visiting a Jívaro household on the Río Pangui, he will say that his home group is the *kaŋaim šuarä* (Río Cangaimi people). If he is visiting another tribe, such as the Achuara, he will use an even broader term to denote his own people, e.g., *untsuri šuarä* (numerous people), a term encompassing all the people who speak his dialect, in other words, the Jívaro tribe, but even its boundaries may be somewhat hazy in his mind. Given the haziness of definition of community and an absence of uni-lineal kin groups, the household tends to be the most concrete social unit visible in Jívaro society.

The Household, Child-rearing, and Kin

Most Jívaro households are very close-knit economic and social units, in contrast to the neighborhood and tribal society as a whole. Each house, averaging about nine occupants, is usually isolated a half-mile or more from the next; but sometimes two, or rarely three, houses may be located within three hundred yards of one another. Adjacent houses, when they occur, invariably belong to close relatives, usually one being that of a middle-aged man and the other(s) of his son(s)-in-law. Even such limited concentrations are not very permanent, due to such factors as quarreling between the neighboring relatives or the gradual depletion of the local wild game supply.

A household tends to have a typical composition of: one

man, two wives, and seven children; or a man, one wife, and three children. Often another relative, such as the widowed mother or an unmarried brother of the head of the household, also resides in the dwelling. Upon marriage of a daughter, the house's population is augmented by the son-in-law (*awe*), who will tend to remain until the birth of his wife's first child. Thereafter, according to the norm, the son-in-law and his family dwell in a new house nearby.

Sometimes matrilocal residence is avoided altogether when the suitor substitutes the gift of a shotgun to his father-in-law, instead of performing the more common bride-service. This substitution of bride-price for bride-service tends to occur in cases where the suitor feels that a period of matrilocal residence would be a liability, rather than an asset to him, e.g., when his bride's family lives in a neighborhood containing a number of enemies of the suitor's family or when he is already married and must take his bride home with him.

The man is formally head of the household and also informally seems generally to dominate his family. He is responsible for protecting his wife (wives) and children, for hunting and fishing, for clearing the forest for garden plots, and for cutting and bringing in fire logs. He also does some very limited garden chores and weaves the family's home-made garments. His wife (wives) is responsible for the overwhelming majority of the agricultural tasks, as well as for cooking and beer preparation, pottery making, and tending the children, chickens, and pigs, if any. When a son-in-law is resident in the household or living nearby, he helps his father-in-law at his various tasks, and also contributes game and firewood to his father-in-law's household. The son-in-law's wife also often helps her mother, even when resident in another neighboring house. A man and his son(s)-in-law normally consider themselves mutually obligated to defend each other's households from enemies.

Men strongly prefer to have two or more wives. The subsistence productivity of the household closely correlates with the number of wives possessed by a man, because the women are responsible for most of the agricultural production. Thus, a satisfactory household production of food and the important manioc beer is dependent upon polygyny.

The most common number of wives for a man to have is two, one, or three, in that order. The emphasis on polygyny, in part, reflects the fact that the ratio of adult females to adult males is approximately 2:1, largely as a consequence of the attrition of the adult male population through killing. The demand for wives nevertheless exceeds the supply, as evidenced by the common practice of "reserving" a pre-puberty girl as a future wife by giving gifts of featherwork and trade goods to her parents. Not infrequently, her future husband then takes her home with him to raise her in his house prior to the actual consummation of the marriage. The extreme nature of the demand for wives is illustrated by the fact that men sometimes get a pregnant woman and her husband to agree to "reserve" the unborn child for him if it should be female. Needless to say, these practices result in marriages in which the husband is often substantially older.

An unmarried girl of post-puberty age is normally courted and involved in the decision to become a wife. The suitor, after he informally ascertains her willingness, sends a close male kinsman of his own generation to act as a go-between to sound out the girl's father who, in turn, consults with the girl and her mother. If the go-between reports back to the suitor that there is no opposition, then the latter goes late one afternoon to the house of the girl and her parents, and sleeps that night in the men's end of the house. Before dawn, he leaves the house with a blowgun and goes hunting, attempting to kill a large number of birds and monkeys in order to impress the girl's parents with his competence. When he returns, he offers the game to the girl to cook and he awaits her final decision. If she has decided to marry him, she will squat down beside the suitor when she serves the cooked food and join him in eating it. From that moment on, they are considered husband and wife and will sleep together that night.

The importance of wives in producing food and beer goes far beyond the subsistence requirements of the household itself. Plural wives assure a surplus production which will make possible adequate entertainment of visitors from other households. The Jívaro place a high value on drinking beer and eating (perhaps in that order), so that one's status in a neighborhood is greatly affected by one's generosity with beer and food. No one can expect to have many friends unless he is a good host; and he cannot easily meet the requirements of good hospitality without plural wives as a labor force.

A man also prefers to have plural wives so that one will be available to accompany him when he goes hunting while the other(s) tends the household and garden. The wife who goes with him not only handles the dog and acts as the intermediary with Nuŋuí, but also assists him by carrying a machete and a basket of manioc and other provisions. Usually the preferred companion for such hunting trips is the youngest wife, who is least likely to be encumbered with children and therefore most willing to go. The wife often looks forward to hunting trips as an opportunity to have sexual intercourse in privacy, away from the rest of the household. Having sexual relations on the hunt is, however, viewed as dangerous by the man, it being believed that after intercourse he is particularly susceptible to being bitten by a poisonous snake. Nevertheless, men often engage in sexual activity when they take their wives hunting.

Men also claim that they would rather go hunting than to engage in sexual relations with the possible consequence of pregnancy, since babies interfere with the mobility of their wives to accompany them in hunting. Therefore, men usually state that they are reluctant to engage in sexual intercourse more often than about once every six to eight days. Field observations, of course, were difficult to make on this point, but my impression is that these particular statements were not too inconsistent with their behavior. Men also believe that having more than one wife decreases, rather than increases, the likelihood of reproduction. The reasoning is that a second wife permits a man to spend more time hunting and thus reduces the frequency of his acts of sexual intercourse. The arduous, mountainous travel required in hunting may also, in itself, divert potential sexual energies.

While many young wives seem to prefer the childless situation which makes it easy for them to go hunting with their husbands, an attempt at contraception is usually only made by single lovers. The attempt essentially employs sympathetic magic rather than herbs and only is believed to work if the male partner is a shaman. The girl brings him a raw chicken egg, he blows on it, and she swallows the egg while he holds her head underwater in a stream. This act is specific only to the young man, and is believed to prevent the girl forever from being impregnated by him. No vegetal abortives of any kind are known.

Women often do want children and, if no conception takes

place after a long period of time, may resort to an anti-
sterility remedy, which consists of the pulverized leg bone of
a fox, which is mixed with manioc beer and drunk. Both men
and women say that the preferred first child is a boy, which
is justified on the basis that the father needs, and would en-
joy having, a son to go hunting with him. Ideally, the birth
of a son should be followed by that of a daughter. There is
no clear-cut prejudice against offspring of one sex as against
the other.

The Jívaro are aware of the relationship between insemina-
tion and pregnancy, and predict that a fully mature woman
can give birth to a baby when the *naitka* tree (botanical
identification unknown) has flowered three times after her
marriage. The *naitka* flowers twice a year, so their estimate
is a year and a half. If the bride is just barely past puberty,
they estimate that a longer period, five *naitka*, or two and a
half years, is required.

Since premarital sexual relations are common, the birth of a
child in a shorter period after marriage is not a cause for
surprise. After the birth of the first baby, a three *naitka*
minimum is estimated for the next.

It is recognized that pregnant women have strange food
cravings and may practice geophagy, something never done
by anyone else in the society. They may eat, in small amounts,
unfired pottery clay or the brown earth from tubular, above-
ground anthills. When birth is expected within five days or
so, the woman's diet is restricted to exclude the meat of
certain wild birds.

Preparation for the birth primarily consists of placing two
stout forked sticks, supporting a crossbar about two and a half
feet above the ground, in the expectant mother's garden. At
the time of birth, a clean banana leaf is placed under the

crossbar, and the mother squats on it with her arms hanging over the bar. Two persons assist her, ideally her husband and her mother. One holds her arms down over the crossbar and the other gets behind her and helps to work the baby down and out to fall on the banana leaf. If it is raining, the birth takes place in the house, but the garden is otherwise preferred by the mother for privacy, because she is "embarrassed."

No couvade is observed by the new father. Rather, he can go forth daily to hunt game and, if he has no other wife, he takes on the responsibility of fetching water, digging up the manioc in the garden, washing it in the stream, and carrying it into the house. There it is cooked by his recuperating wife, who is not supposed to undertake other household or garden tasks for about two weeks. If she should fail to rest adequately for such a period, it is believed that she will be bedridden for a long time, due to becoming sick from "handling cold water," such as when washing the manioc. In order to protect the health of the baby, both parents observe certain dietary restrictions, such as avoiding eating any birds that forage close to the ground, or consuming the entrails of any animal. It is also believed that if either parent engages in extramarital sexual relations during the child's infancy, the infant will die, vomiting.

When the baby is a few days old, it is given a mild hallucinogenic drug, *tsentsemä* (botanically unidentified). The uncooked leaf of this plant, which can be used by persons of all ages, is masticated and fed to the infant, whether male or female. The purpose of the administration of this hallucinogen is to help the baby possibly to see *arutam* (see pp. 135–43), and thus get supernatural power to help its survival. If the baby becomes sick, the drug may be given again.

The child is given a name within a few days after being

born. In some families, the father names both sons and
daughters; but in others, the father may give the boys their
names and the mother may bestow the names on the girls.
If the father's father or the mother's mother are still alive,
they may be asked to name the child of their own sex. In any
event, ideally the child should be named for a deceased
relative of the parental or grandparental generation on either
side of the family who, if male, was respected for killing
and working hard and, if female, respected for working hard.
The names are often those of animals, especially birds, while
many others have no meaning other than as names. Within a
few days of naming, both the male and female infants have
their ears pierced.

Infanticide is regularly practiced only in the case of de-
formed children. It is accomplished by crushing the infant
with a foot. Sometimes unmarried girls kill their "illegiti-
mate" babies immediately upon birth if they have no expecta-
tion of marrying the father. Infanticide of undeformed babies
by married women seems to be unheard of. Birth of twins is
never a reason for infanticide.

After the first two weeks or so, the new mother returns
to the garden. The work there is arduous, involving much
squatting and stooping in connection with harvesting manioc
and, especially, weeding. As a result, she normally leaves the
infant at home in a small hammock by her bed. Since the
garden work takes many hours of her day, the baby often becomes hungry and cries a great deal without getting attention.
If there is a daughter approximately four years of age or more
in the household, the baby's mother will ask her to tend it.
When the infant cries considerably, the baby-tender will pick
it up and sing to it. Not surprisingly, the typical lullaby
among the Jívaro is not sung by the mother, but by a female

child, and the words of it are addressed to the mother to come back from the garden to nurse the infant:

> Dear mother, dear mother
> Come soon, come soon.
> The baby is crying,
> The baby is crying.
> For lack of your milk,
> It will die.
> For lack of your milk,
> It will die.
> Dear mother, come quickly,
> Dear mother, come quickly,
> The little monkey is singing,
> The little monkey is singing.

Often the mother does not return for several hours, and the baby-tender often attempts to satisfy the infant's hunger by chewing up boiled manioc and spitting it into the baby's mouth. Any other mothers in the household who may be lactating do not offer to feed the baby, and wet-nursing is unknown. If a mother finds herself unable to provide the baby with enough milk, she feeds it masticated manioc or a bit of beer.

When the baby begins teething it will also be fed steamed hearts of palm with a consistency softer than that of boiled noodles. Small bits of chewed meat are provided soon thereafter.

The birth of a new baby normally does not entail the weaning of the earlier one, and it is a common sight to see an infant and a four- or five-year-old being fed by the mother, with one at each breast. Puppies are highly valued and cared for by the women, and one may likewise be seen being breast-fed simultaneously by a woman along with her own infant. Weaning is not emphasized and may not take place until the child is six or seven years old. The mother may accomplish this by putting a mildly hot pepper on her nipples. If that has little effect, she has recourse to a hotter variety.

The infant is wrapped loosely in a piece of cloth, which is taken off and used, with water, to wipe the child clean of excrement. The cloth is then washed and dried over a fire for reuse. A baby's excessive crying may be interpreted as evidence that it is "very hot," i.e., has a fever, and the mother may bathe it in lukewarm water to cool the child sufficiently so that it will fall asleep. Sometimes a mother, on being awakened by a baby's crying, will scold and strike it in anger.

To teach the child to walk, the father lashes a stave railing around the three open sides of the mother's bed to create a simple "crib" which the child can grasp for support.

The attitude toward toilet training is quite relaxed. When a toddler starts to defecate or urinate in the house, it is taken outside; but it is not castigated verbally or otherwise. The mother simply digs up the soiled portion of the dirt floor and throws it out. The simplicity of this solution, together with the fact that adults themselves may urinate on the floor at night to avoid exposing themselves to possible attackers outside the house, helps one understand their attitude. Later, the child is simply told to go outside, but if it fails to do so, there is no condemnatory admonition. Finally, however, if the child is still failing to go out of the house by the time it is about five years old, then the mother will speak her disapproval. As a last resort, she may spank the child lightly with a vine.

Children are encouraged to wash their hands and to bathe. They are told that if they do not wash their hands before eating, their growth will be delayed and stunted. Girls are told, in addition, that they must wash their hands before preparing beer or else the product will not be satisfactory. It is believed that if children are not taught to bathe at an early age, they will be afraid of cold water and their parents will find it necessary to drag them to the stream. Getting the child used to bathing is also seen as connected with teaching it, in the process, to swim well, a skill which is considered essential to survival because of the frequent necessity of crossing streams and rivers which are often dangerously swollen and rapid.

Children tend to be discouraged from playing, since it is felt that such behavior leads to a disinclination to work. Jesting or joking by children is similarly frowned upon, because it is believed to lead to lying in adult life. Nonetheless, children do often try to play until halted by their parents, who are likely to stop them more rapidly if children of both sexes are playing together. If a particular older child, who is visiting, has a reputation for playing and jesting, parents may tell their own offspring not to play with the visitor.

At this point, it seems appropriate to point out that one of the more significant features of Jívaro socialization may be the relative isolation of children from peers outside their own polygynous nuclear family, due to the extreme dispersion of households in the forest. This isolation seems likely to be conducive to a sense of alienation from the rest of the tribe, particularly when coupled with the traditional early morning lectures which fathers give to "make them be careful" in dealing with others beyond the household and which emphasize the deceitful and treacherous characteristics of other tribesmen. Adding to the child's sense of insecurity vis-à-vis the rest of the population is the frequent attribution of illness within the household to the bewitching activities of hostile shamans. Finally, the dispersion of the population in small households over a large area results in a very poor communication system in which fourth- or fifth-hand information usually arrives garbled and exaggerated through repetition, the erroneous rumors giving rise to misunderstanding, suspicion, and hostility.

Children frequently steal portions of cooked meat from one another and wrestle over them, which reflects the fact that meat is not always abundant in the household, depending on the father's hunting success and his immediate commitment to some other task, such as clearing trees. There is also a reluctance to give a small child more than a single piece of meat, for it is believed that varying the portion may cause it to cry when it doesn't get as much as it did on a previous occasion.

While stealing and wrestling over meat is disapproved of and, if repeated, may be punished by the father by spanking with a nettle, wrestling for its own sake between boys is approved and encouraged, although the father may advise them not to hurt one another. Sometimes nettle spanking may be used to stop children from playing, or the father may find it sufficient simply to threaten to bring a nettle. A child who regularly grabs things that he might damage, such as pottery bowls, may have his hand beaten with a nettle. In general, however, there is little in the Jívaro house that a child can damage, since pottery not in use is stored on high bamboo shelves, and personal effects are suspended in baskets out of their reach. As a result, discipline with regard to safeguarding property is not emphasized.

If a child is extraordinarily bad, and, despite nettle spanking, continues breaking pottery vessels, taking meat without asking permission, and stealing peanuts from storage baskets above the rafters, the parents may undertake the harshest punishment they ever use on children. This consists of dropping a large quantity of hot peppers into a small fire and forcing the child to remain over the fire under a large cloth until he becomes unconscious. When he recovers, he may be admonished that if he again misbehaves, he will have all his hair burned off. However, this threat apparently is never carried out.

A much more subtle method of disciplining children consists of administering the juice of the *maikua* (*Datura arborea*) plant to them. This action is usually taken when a child is disrespectful of his father and calls into question his knowledge and authority. As one informant put it, "Only some sons obey their fathers. Some say, 'The old man is very old—he doesn't know what he is talking about.' It was like this in the oldtime, too." The administration of this particularly strong hallucinogenic extract is designed to put him into a trance state to see the supernatural world. It is believed that there he will discover that many of the claims the father has been making about the nature of reality are true and he will be less disrespectful. In addition, the hallucinogenic experience may put him in contact with an *arutam* (see pp. 135–43), and this also is seen as a possible bonus for the development of his character. This is a culture where a parent may threaten to give a child a hallucinogenic drug if it misbehaves.

The use of hallucinogens in child-rearing is by no means restricted to disciplinary problems. As has been noted earlier, the relatively mild *tsentsemä* is given to a new-born infant. If the child is female, *tsentsemä* is again administered, with a little tobacco water, when she is between about two and eight years old. Her parents hope she may acquire *arutam* soul power and thus be able, when she grows older, to work hard and have success in reproducing children, raising crops, chickens, and pigs. She is administered the drug within the

1. View of the middle Río Upano north of Huambi,
looking eastward (1956–57).

2. Side view of a Jívaro house and its surrounding garden
(upper Río Yuquipa region, 1956–57).

3. Man taking time out from land clearing to play a flute (Río Sepa, 1956–57).

4. Woman carrying gourd water container and a basket of freshly peeled sweet manioc roots (Río Sepa, 1956–57).

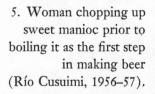

5. Woman chopping up sweet manioc prior to boiling it as the first step in making beer (Río Cusuimi, 1956–57).

6. Stirring the boiled manioc with a wooden paddle. This is done in conjunction with mastication to prepare the mash for fermentation (Río Sepa, 1956–57).

7. Mashing chonta palm fruits with a wooden mortar and pestle preparatory to making chonta fruit beer. The metal cup is the author's (Río Cusuimi, 1956–57).

8. Hunter returning home with a howler monkey which he shot with a blowgun (on his right shoulder) and poisoned darts (Río Cusuimi, 1956–57).

9. Jaguar skin being dried for trade to the frontier Jívaro (region between the upper Río Macuma and the upper Río Cangaimi, 1956–57).

10. Man (left) and wife sleeping in a new house, in which the walls are still under construction (Río Cusuimi, 1956–57).

11. Hunting dogs tied to beds to sound the alarm in case would-be assassins attempt to approach sleeping members of the household in the night (Río Cusuimi, 1956–57).

context of a four-day feast and dance, *uči auk* ("child swallowing"), in which approximately half a dozen such girls participate together. Prior to the event the girls observe dietary restrictions for about a week, not eating the meat of any mammals or birds. The ceremonies take place in and near the house of the host, a father of one of the girls. On the first day the girls dance until midafternoon. Then they are given *tsentsemä* and are taken at nightfall to palm thatch lean-to's in the adjacent forest, where they will lie down to have visions and dreams of bountiful crops, chickens, and pigs. Meanwhile, the adults dance and drink in the house until dawn. The same procedure is repeated for three additional nights.

The most important use of hallucinogens in child-rearing, from the Jívaro point of view, is to assist a boy in seeing an *arutam* at a sacred waterfall, since his life is believed to depend upon it. This will be discussed in detail later (see pp. 135–39). Of all a boy's childhood experiences, nothing is considered to compare in importance with the experience. The power deriving from the acquired *arutam* soul is seen in Jívaro terms as an enculturating and socializing device, since its force is believed to promote almost all the value aspects of character, including honesty, inclination to work, and intelligence; as well as to increase the actual knowledge of the child.

Training in work and skills conforms to the adult sexual division of labor. A girl from about the age of four to six is not expected to do much more than care for the baby, if any, while the mother is working in the garden or preparing beer in the house. She is instructed, among other things, to keep the infant from eating dirt and from being bitten by ants, and to rock it in its hammock. She is also supposed to sweep the house floor at least daily and throw out the accumulation of refuse. If there is no infant, this will probably be her only duty.

A girl approximately six years or older may have not only the above tasks, but also directly assists her mother in garden work of all kinds, including planting, weeding, and harvesting. When her mother is making pottery, she imitates her by making and firing miniature vessels and also may form and fire miniature dogs. No dolls in human form are produced, however. A boy who may be tempted to work with clay is discouraged by his father, who advises him not to touch it or else the boy's penis will one day stay soft and limp like a coil of clay.

A boy, when about four, begins to learn the art of blowgun hunting. His father gives him a small hollow reed less than a foot long and makes little darts. The child, who at that age tags along after his mother to the garden, uses it to shoot at butterflies. When he is about six, his father presents him with a real miniature blowgun and a dart quiver. Then, while his mother works in the garden, he wanders about, shooting at the hummingbirds coming to feed at the flowers of the manioc plants. Those that he kills, he brings to her to cook, which she does gravely. He is not allowed to eat them himself, it being believed that he cannot kill again if he does so. By approximately nine years of age, his skill normally has advanced to the stage that he is killing larger birds lurking in the trees around the garden. His father then takes him hunting and gives him his first formal instruction in killing game, and has him assist by carrying it home. In the house, the father encourages the development of other male skills by showing approval when the son attempts to make miniature baskets or model houses and rafts.

Post-puberty boys perform most of the tasks of their

fathers, including participation in the defense of the house and in attacks on enemies. A son may accompany his father on a raid as early as the age of six; but it is more common for this to happen when he is nine or older.

When a boy reaches the age of about sixteen, he formally undertakes to establish his adult status by going into the forest, killing a tree sloth, and making a *tsantsa* of its head (for the supernatural reasons, see pp. 143–49). Then two *tsantsa* feasts of celebration are given by the father or other older male relative in which all the ritual precautions of the human head *tsantsa* celebration are observed, although the feasting is not as lavish.

With the second feast, the transition of the head-taker into adult life is implicitly recognized, and he is now entitled to wear the *etsemat*, the basic headpiece of Jívaro men, consisting of a long cotton band with a red and yellow toucan feather tassel (see Plates 12–15). The donning of this headband has significant overtones since it is used by men not only to keep their hair in place but also in war to hang a human head from the shoulder. He may also now carve a round stool for himself, although he usually does not do this until, or unless, he has participated in a regular killing expedition. Finally, the giving of the feasts means that he is entitled to get married, but he probably will not actually do this until he is about twenty-one to twenty-three years old.

A somewhat analogous pair of feasts is given as puberty celebrations for a girl. Both feasts are sponsored by the girl's father, the first being a minor affair of two days' length; the second being given about half a year later, after her family has been able to accumulate enough chickens and pigs to feed a large number of guests for six or seven days. The supernatural aspect of this "coming out" celebration centers around the girl drinking water mixed with crushed green tobacco leaves in order to enter the supernatural world while sleeping in a nearby lean-to and to have dreams that will augur success in raising garden crops and domesticated animals. The feasts are known as *nua tsaŋu* (woman tobacco) or *kasakü.*

Polygyny is preferred in the sororal form because sisters are reputed to get along better with one another. A man normally hopes that his father-in-law (*iči*) eventually will give him all the latter's daughters as wives. Accordingly, the son-in-law's conscientious post-marital bride-service is usually performed to keep his wife's father favorably impressed, so that he will provide such additional brides. Thus men occasionally may obtain several sisters as wives. In such cases, the man is assured of an outstanding production of beer and food and, presumably, a relatively tranquil polygynous family.

Wives who are sisters usually work out a hierarchical relationship, with the eldest (characteristically the first bride) assuming direction of activities within the house. The second wife, likewise, somewhat dominates the third, and so on. Still, each wife has her own section of the garden which she exclusively works, her own cook-fire, bed, and pottery vessels. Not uncommonly, when a man marries a widow who has an unmarried daughter, the daughter will eventually, and casually, become his second wife. In such cases of stepdaughter marriage, the mother tends to retain a relatively dominant position over her daughter. The situation is usually more individualistic in the case of wives who are not sisters or mothers and daughters. These tend to be too antagonistic to submit to a consistent dominant-subordinate relationship in household activities.

The most difficult situation tends to occur when a husband brings home a new wife who is not a sister of his pre-existing wife (wives). Since he is already married, he cannot practice temporary matrilocality at the house of his new wife's parents, and thus he must introduce her into a household where the other adult female(s) will tend to be antagonistic. Usually the husband attempts to bring the bride in unannounced so as to take his other wife (wives) by surprise, and tries to act as though the new wife is just a routine addition to the household. Reportedly, however, it is common for an irate pre-existing wife to unleash a temper tantrum, throwing pottery vessels and other handy artifacts at the husband. She may also soon be engaging in quarrels and hair-pullings with the new addition, but normally life in the dwelling gradually settles down, particularly after the new wife has a baby.

The only kinswoman with whom marriage is formally sanctioned is a cross-cousin (*wahe*) from either parent's side of the family. A man does have the alternative of finding a marriage partner outside of his kindred, but this normally requires him to move out of his home neighborhood (because of the practice of temporary matrilocality) and consequently to live among strangers who may be intent on killing him for some earlier wrong by one of his kinsmen or simply because he took one of their own preferred potential mates. Slightly over half of actual marriages are with cross-cousins.

With the normatively unrestricted practice of polygyny creating a high demand for unattached women throughout interior Jívaro society, the preference for cross-cousin marriage promotes conflict in the nuclear family when brothers become old enough to marry, for they all share the same few preferred mates. Not surprisingly, many of the disputes among kinsmen thus arise between brothers over the question of wife acquisition, and the practice of matrilocal residence tends to isolate the brothers from one another. In fact, the norm is for a man to side with his *iči* (father-in-law and father of cross-cousins) and *sai* (wife's brother and male cross-cousins) in disputes against his own consanguineal relatives. The potential reward of obtaining more daughters as wives from his father-in-law often acts as an additional, but unspoken, inducement for a man to take the side of his in-laws in a quarrel.

By the time a man is ready to seek a female cross-cousin (*wahe*), her father may be dead, and he thus commonly must instead ask her brother (his *sai*) for her. Since there is a scarcity of marriageable women, it is common for her brother to demand reciprocity as part of the agreement, i.e., an exchange of sisters for marriage. Such an arrangement has the advantage of entailing none of the bride-service obligations which would be due the bride's father if he were alive, and of not requiring the normal temporary matrilocal residence at the bride's father's house, which may be in a "dangerous" neighborhood for the groom. As a by-product, the sister exchange also can cement friendly relations between cross-cousins of the same generation, as may be seen in the following case described by one informant:

Tukupï and Ašaŋä are male cross-cousins [*sai*]. Tukupï had an unmarried sister, Nampirä. Ašaŋä asked Tukupï for her (the father of Tukupï and Nampirä was dead). Tukupï gave her to Ašaŋä, and Ašaŋä and Nampirä became husband and wife. But then Ašaŋä did not want to give *his own* sister to Tukupï. Also Ašaŋä frequently beat Nampirä when he got drunk.

So Tukupï went to the house of Ašaŋä. He said, "Why do you beat my sister? If you want to hit my sister, then hit me."

They began to fight (wrestling and hitting each other with pieces of wood). Then Tukupï left. Thereafter, whenever they met, they fought. Finally, Ašaŋä gave his sister to Tukupï. Thereafter, when Ašaŋä beat Tukupï's sister, Tukupï beat Ašaŋä's sister.

Tukupï said, "Before, when you beat my sister, I went to fight you. But now that you have given me your sister, I will beat her instead."

So now everything is friendly between Tukupï and Ašaŋa.

Joking relationships are restricted to cross-cousins, with emphasis on humor between cross-cousins of the opposite sex, who frequently banter flirtatiously with each other. The jokes are often explicit sexual challenges, even between persons married to others and, when engaged in by elderly cross-cousins, are often the occasion for general mirth in the household. The Jívaro explain that they cannot joke with other relatives because of their "respect" for them. The highest degree of such respect is shown by a man to his mother-in-law, from whom he averts his eyes when speaking with her. For a man to look directly into the eyes of a woman, even in conversation, is considered flirtatious behavior, and for him to look into the eyes of another man is considered a hostile act.

Beyond the polygynous nuclear family, the basic Jívaro kin group is a personal bilateral kindred with a slight patrilineal tendency. The personal bilateral kindred, however, should not even be referred to as a "group," for as Murdock has noted,[2] a person shares an identical kindred only with his siblings and even then only before marriage. Since each person has a different kindred, his personal kin rights and obligations can coincide only with those of siblings of the same sex. Classification of kinsmen is by degrees of distance from one's self (ego), rather than in terms of membership or nonmembership in some sort of corporate unit, as is commonly found in unilineal descent societies. The Jívaro thus possess the most insecure of the basic types of kinship systems, and lack clearly defined descent groups which can protect their members from outside enemies and which can settle disputes among relatives.

The Jívaro version of the kindred seems even more insecure than most for the individual, for in disputes any serious reckoning of kinship is a source of considerable confusion, involving disagreements over degree of relatedness, even in the case of a single person. In any serious discussion of kin obligations among the Jívaro, all single-word, or elementary, kin terms of reference have added to them the modifier "true" (*nekás*) or "branch" (*kaná*) to pin down degrees of relationship (see Table 1 and Figure 2 for the elementary kinship terms). In the case of any specific relative, these modifying terms can often be substituted for one another, depending upon the degree of closeness of relationship which the speaker wishes to recognize in a given situation. The only kin always defined as "true" relatives are a person's biological grandparents, parents, siblings, children, cross-cousins, and fathers of his cross-cousins. The only relatives who are always assigned to the "branch" category are affinal kin who, prior to marrying, were not considered by *ego* to be relatives of any degree. Since definition of degree of kinship is thus commonly manipulated at will, a person is often uncertain as to how his relatives will define their obligations and rights in any given dispute. The use of these "true" and "branch" modifiers almost doubles the varieties of relationship distinguished, so that many of the relatives in the kindred are unlikely to be defined as precisely the same, even by two siblings, in any particular crisis.

TABLE I
KINSHIP: ELEMENTARY TERMS OF
REFERENCE AND TERMS OF ADDRESS

Key to abbreviations

Br	brother	Gs	grandson
Da	daughter	Hu	husband
Fa	father	Mo	mother
Gc	grandchild	Si	sister
Gd	granddaughter	So	son
Gp	grandparent	Wi	wife

The abbreviations also represent the possessive form; thus, MoBrDaSo is mother's brother's daughter's son.

O   a formerly more common term
N   a recently innovated term
A   a term recently borrowed from the Achuara

MALE SPEAKING; TERMS OF ADDRESS
IN PARENTHESES

FaFa, MoFa *apači*   also GpBr   (*apači* O; *apáčiru* O)

FaMo, MoMo *nukuči*   also GpSi   (*nukuči* O; *nukučiči* N)

Fa, FaBr, MoSiHu   *apa*   (*apawa; apačï; apawači; apa* N A)

Mo, MoSi, MoBrWi, FaSi, FaBrWi   *nuku* (*nukuači; nukúa*);
  if *ego* marries a daughter of MoBrWi, FaSi, or FaBrWi,
  tsatsa (*nukúa*) is substituted for *nuku* with regard to the
  bride's mother.

FaSiHu, MoBr, WiFa   *iči*   (*iči*)

Br, FaBrSo, FaSiDaHu, MoSiSo, MoBrDaHu   *yači*   *yatsuči*—younger to older brother; *umpá*—older to younger)

Si, FaBrDa, FaSiSoWi, MoSiDa, MoBrSoWi   *umaí* (*makú;
  umači* N; *umaimi* O; *umaímiči* O; *umáčiru*)

SiHu, FaSiSo, FaBrDaHu, MoBrSo, MoSiDaHu, WiBr
  sai   (*saikma*)

BrWi, FaSiDa, FaBrSoWi, MoBrDa, MoSiSoWi   *wahe* (*umačí*)

So, BrSo, FaBrSoSo, FaSiDaSo, FaBrDaDaHu, FaSiSoDaHu, MoSiSoSo, MoBrDaSo, SiDaHu, MoSiDaDaHu, MoBrSo- DaHu   *uči* (*umpá; sukí* O; *aišmaŋči* O; *aišmaŋá* O; *aiš- maŋru* O)

Da, BrDa, FaBrSoDa, FaSiDaDa, FaBrDaSoWi, FaSiSoSoWi, MoSiSoDa, MoBrDaDa, SiSoWi, MoSiDaSoWi, MoBrSo- SoWi   *nawanta* (*makú; makuči*)

DaHu, BrDaHu, SiSo, FaBrDaSo, FaSiSoSo, FaBrSoDaHu, FaSi- DaDaHu, MoSiDaSo, MoBrSoSo, MoSiSoDaHu, MoBrDa- DaHu   *awe* (*aweči; awetá*)

SoWi, BrSoWi, SiDa, FaBrDaDa, FaSiSoDa, FaBrSoSoWi, FaSi- DaSoWi, MoSiDaDa, MoBrSoDa, MoSiSoSoWi, MoBrDa- SoWi   *awe* (*aweči; awetá*)

Gs, Gd, Gc   *tiraŋi*   (*tiraŋi; tiraŋči*)

Wi   *ekentu; nua*   (*ekenturu* O).   First wife: *tarimta.* Second wife: *učič nua.* Third wife: *yamaí nuatčmu.*

FEMALE SPEAKING; TERMS OF ADDRESS IN PARENTHESES

Terms are the same as for male speaking, except for the fol- lowing:

Br, FaBrSo, FaSiDaHu, MoSiSo, MoBrDaHu   *umaí* (*umači* N; *umaimi* O; *umaímiči* O; *umáčiru*)

Si, FaBrDa, FaSiSoWi, MoSiDa, MoBrSoWi   *kai* (*kaičiru, kaiči*—younger to older sister; *makú*—older to younger)

SiHu, FaSiSo, FaBrDaHu, MoBrSo, MoSiDaHu   *wahe* (*umači*)

BrWi, FaSiDa, FaBrSoWi, MoBrDa, MoSiSoWi   *yua* (*yuači; yuamči; yuačiru*)

So, BrSo, FaBrSoSo, FaSiDaSo, MoSiSoSo, MoBrDaSo, SiSo, FaBrDaSo, FaSiSoSo, MoSiDaSo, MoBrSoSo   *uči* (*aeš- maŋá; áešmaŋru*)

DaHu, BrDaHu, FaBrSoDaHu, FaSiDaDaHu, MoSiSoDaHu, MoBrDaDaHu, FaBrDaDaHu, FaSiSoDaHu, SiDaHu, MoSi-DaDaHu, MoBrSoDaHu   *awe* N (*aweči* N; *awetá* N; *antepá* O) *Awe* has replaced *antepä*, the male-speaking term of reference being adopted.

Da, BrDa, FaBrSoDa, FaSiDaDa, MoSiSoDa, MoBrDaDa, Br-SoWi, SiDa, FaBrDaDa, FaSiSoDa, FaBrSoSoWi, FaSiDa-SoWi, MoSiDaDa, MoBrSoDa, MoSiSoSoWi, MoBrDa-SoWi   *nawanta* (*makú; makuči*)

SoWi, SiSoWi, FaBrDaSoWi, FaSiSoSoWi, MoSiDaSoWi, Mo-BrSoSoWi   *nahatï* O(*naháturu* O; *makú; aweči* N; *awetá* N) *Nahatï* is beginning to be replaced by *awe*, the male-speaking term of reference being adopted.

Hu   *aeš* (*áeširu*)

Co-wives are normally referred to by the *kai* term.

The utilization of these "true" and "branch" modifiers may be somewhat clarified by a few examples. According to the kinship rules, *ego* is expected to side with a true relative in a dispute with a branch relative of the same elementary category. However, *ego* must often decide at the time which of the two disputants is the "true" one and therefore deserving of his aid. No matter whose side *ego* decides to join, the abandoned party may be expected to accuse him of not living up to his kinship obligations. If *ego* does not join either party in the dispute, then both tend to level that accusation at him.

Similarly, another relative may manipulate the terminology when *ego* requests help from him. *Ego* may request aid from a parallel cousin, for example, saying, "You are my true 'brother' (*nekás yači*) and therefore you must help me in my dispute against this man who is only your branch 'brother-in-law' (*kaná sai*)." If the parallel cousin does not wish to accede to the request, he replies, "I wish I could help you, but

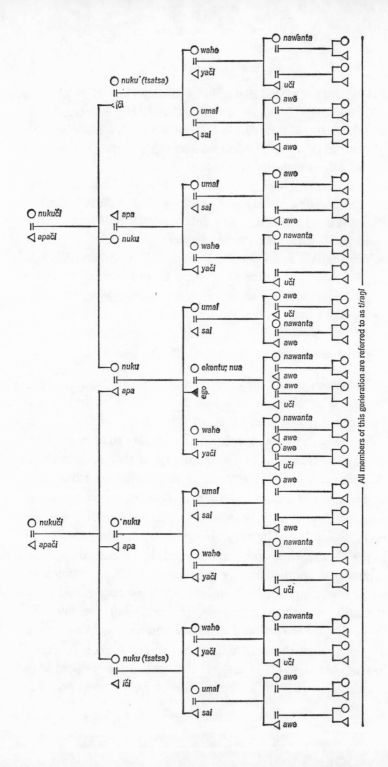

you are mistaken. You are really my branch 'brother' (*kaná yači*), not my true 'brother,' and since this enemy of yours is really my true 'brother-in-law' (*nekás sai*) it would not be right."

Although often a source of frustration and confusion, this manipulation of defined degree of relationship can serve to save a man's life. When he visits a strange house, the host may subject him to an interrogation regarding the names of his relatives and their degree of relationship to the visitor, pretending a purely friendly interest in the subject. Usually, however, the host really wants to determine whether his visitor is a close relative of any of his enemies. In answering his interrogator, the visitor carefully puts into the "branch" category as many of his relatives as possible, particularly those whom he thinks may be enemies of the host. At the same time, he promotes to the "true" category those of his relatives whom he knows are friendly to the interrogator or the interrogator's relatives. A good memory of kin relationships of both enemies and friends is, of course, essential to this sometimes adroit manipulation of the "true–branch" definitions.

Failure to manipulate kin classification successfully can result in the visitor's food or beer being poisoned or in his being ambushed by the host after he leaves the house. It is not surprising, therefore, that fathers often spend an hour or more before dawn lecturing their sons on the degree of relationship between a variety of enemies and friends in their own and other neighborhoods. Such lectures also include advice on how to avoid dangerous entanglements, how to

FIGURE 2 (*facing page*)
Kinship Chart. Elementary terms of reference (male speaking)

get along well with kinsmen, and how to survive in general, as illustrated by this excerpt from such a morning monologue:

Listen, son, when you grow up, do not enter the house of Ampušä, who is my enemy. When I die, when my daughter is grown, she can marry whom she wants. If her husband is from a distant neighborhood, don't go to visit her. Afterwards, when you have married and I am dead, if you have a daughter, I know that one day the son of my enemy will make peace with you. But don't give him your daughter, or he will kill you. When I die, you have to give your sister to your true [nekás] sai. Thus you will live in peace and there will be no fighting or anything. If you give her to another man, then when you drink beer and get drunk, that man, although he is married to your sister, can speak to my enemy to plot your death. Thus are they accustomed to kill.

Then when your daughter is married, never speak harshly to your *awe* [son-in-law] or get mad at him or he will leave your daughter and become your enemy. When one never gets angry with his *awe*, and lives peacefully, the *awe* divides his game, and also his chickens and pigs, with you. Sometimes, when we get old, we cannot build a house. But if we have an *awe*, he will help build it.

Never beat your wife or get drunk. If some other man sees this happen and talks about it, it will be a shame. If you live well and give your daughter to an *awe*, then the father or brother of this *awe* may come to visit in order to see how you live. If you don't live well together, then the father of this *awe* will say, "This man is bad."

Also you must tell your daughter, "Obey your husband, supply good food, and do not commit adultery with other men. Otherwise he will surely beat you. And if the family of your husband comes to visit, you have to get up immediately and serve beer and food to the guests. If you don't, then they and many other people will say that you don't get up, even though your husband asks you to do so, and this is bad."

When you are living well, thus, with all your *sai* and *yači*, if someone comes and kills your *sai*, you have to avenge him. First of all, you have to bathe in the sacred waterfall, see *arutam*, and then you can kill. If you have not encountered *arutam*, you must not go kill, because you will die. When they kill someone in your family first, then you have to go and kill one of them. You can win by explaining that they killed first and that you are simply avenging his death. In this way, you can win. Also send the message, "If you kill me, my family will kill you." Then they also will say, "Yes, it is true. We cannot continue living and fighting. Let us calm down a bit. Since we are the same people, let us live peacefully. I want to stay in my house. I want to eat well." When they speak thusly, the feuding will end.

Learn to work. Let us work together. Since we have lots of beer, let us work together. Then when I die, you will know how to work. When we kill a pig, let us eat well, because when we die, it is all finished. So let us work well and eat well while we live. When we work, we work until midafternoon. When you are young, you want to work all day. But I tell you, "Enough, enough. It is very late. We have to return to the house and you have to bathe. Then let us eat well."

When I die, how is it going to be with you? Sometimes when another man drinks beer, he gets angry. But this is bad. You must not do this. When you are drinking, take a nap and then you can get up and drink some more. Dance. Never speak harshly, because some men thus start fighting with their *yači*. Don't do this or otherwise when you travel elsewhere the people will know and speak to one another about it. So don't do this, because then this will be a great shame.

Visiting and Parties

Young single men spend a great deal of a time visiting other households where unmarried female cross-cousins (*wahe*) live. Often such visits last two or three weeks, during which the young man will secretly rendezvous frequently with the girl in the garden or adjacent forest to engage in sexual relations. Her parents usually do not pay much attention to the affair as long as it is never mentioned or observed, although a few fathers are exceptional and may beat a daughter who is suspected of such activities simply because the young man is hanging around. Normally, if the girl becomes pregnant, her parents tell her to bring her lover to their house to live as her husband. Then, the next time she sees him, she invites him to become her husband. She may point out that if he refuses, her father will undoubtedly beat her. It is virtually unknown for the lover, if he is single, to refuse to come live with her, in view of the scarcity of unmarried women.

While young single men are the chief philanderers, young married men also commonly have a penchant for such activities. Under the guise of going hunting, they may visit the houses of other men who are also away hunting and arrange to rendezvous regularly with a wife of the absent husband in the forest near the garden. This kind of activity is so common that husbands sometimes build a special kind of *tampunči* "adulterer trap" near the garden of the suspected wife, which is so designed that a bent sapling will strike the unwanted visitor in the stomach or groin. However, this type of *tampunči*, unlike that used against mortal enemies, does not have body-penetrating bamboo spikes.

Married women reportedly respond often with less enthusiasm when approached by a would-be lover who is also married, "because they do not want to share him with other women." Thus, when a young man is visiting a distant neighborhood where he is relatively unknown, and a woman asks him if he is married, he commonly responds negatively.

When a man has a number of wives, his difficulty in preventing them from engaging in extramarital affairs is believed by the Jívaro to be proportional to their numbers. Of one man, who had a record six wives, an informant said, "He must have eyes in the back of his head." A jealous husband, when he leaves the house, sometimes lectures his wives not to engage in sexual relations with any men, saying that he will learn of it if they do. It is not uncommon for such a man to leave a son or daughter in the house to spy on their own mother and to inform him if she speaks to any men.

Extramarital affairs frequently result in the wife's leaving to live as the wife of her lover, which is viewed by the husband as "wife-stealing," one of the most serious Jívaro offenses and one for which the punitive sanction against the wife-taker is death, and against the woman the slashing of her scalp with a machete. To avoid retribution, the couple commonly flees to a distant neighborhood of the tribe, hopefully one which will be too distant for vengeance to be visited upon them. Such cases of wife-stealing and consequent fleeing are so common that they are one of the major reasons given for the wide geographic distribution of persons who are fairly close relatives.

The new couple usually justifies its action on the basis of romantic love, a concept which is strongly developed among the Jívaro. Young men frequently play love songs softly on musical bows at sunset and hope, thereby, magically to cause their sweethearts to think of them, no matter how distant they may be. Love potions are also used, and much of the featherwork, adornment and face painting worn by men is recognized to be designed, in part, to make them attractive to females. Girls and women typically exert less effort to glamorize their appearance, but do frequently wear "perfume bundles" of sweet-smelling seeds against their breasts.

Parties, centering around manioc beer drinking and *hanse-matä*, or social dances, are the main form of regular group interaction with neighbors. Most typically they occur when a man has worked hard for several days felling trees to expand the garden and wishes to invite a few neighbors to spend a night in recreation with him. He instructs his wives to make a large quantity of beer and then during the next few days does much hunting until he has brought home a good quantity of meat (that which is obtained first is roasted and kept dry and unspoiled in a basket high over a fire). By this time the beer has fermented sufficiently, and he goes to the houses of several friendly neighbors who are also usually close relatives.

Such parties, usually on a slightly smaller scale, also can simply occur when another family happens to drop by on an afternoon to visit or stay overnight, if there is a respectable beer supply on hand. In the latter case, when the party is unplanned, a chicken or two may be killed for meat, since the host may not have wild game meat immediately on hand. Planned parties occur when chonta palm fruit is harvested and made into beer, and also to celebrate when someone has survived snakebite.

After the visitors have been drinking and conversing for a few hours, a few flutes and a monkey skin drum will be brought out, and a kind of "jam session" begins. Soon the women put on snail shell dance belts, and the drinkers begin to dance in pairs, males facing females. The woman hops up and down, her shell belt tinkling the rhythm, while her male partner steps back and forth or strolls casually around while beating the drum. As darkness falls, copal torches are lit, and the party often continues until the middle of the night or early morning. As the pairs of men and women dance opposite each other, they sing in a kind of counterpoint, each his own words, which are sometimes improvised. The content is typically romantic and flirtatious, often with an ironic humor. The following are two examples of these *hansematä* songs, the first that of a woman, the second of a man:

> Why are you so near to me?
> For they will come after us.
> This other one
> Who came very close
> Caused me to boil.
> It would be better if you
> Got farther away.
> And what is your name?
> I'm going to be sleeping here on a bed.

> I asked her,
> "Where are you going?"
> She answered me, saying,
> "I go deep into the eastern forest."
> That is what she told me.
> By the way,
> Another truth is that a stone can talk!

While such *hansematä* songs have a courtship function between single persons, they are sung by all the dancers, including married persons dancing with the spouses of others. As the drinking and dancing proceed, flirtatious behavior may become overt, extending to pinching and other familiarities in the dim light. The quantities of beer drunk require frequent exits from the house to urinate, and not uncommonly a female, exiting from the women's end of the house, will rendezvous secretly with a male, who has left from the opposite door, to satisfy a call of nature different from that which was their publicly implied intention. As the drunkenness develops, men may get into arguments over normally repressed grievances or over allegedly flirtatious behavior with someone else's wife. Wrestling may ensue, or even hitting with a convenient palm wood slat. However, most parties do not involve such unpleasantness and end rather calmly as some of the participants pass out from drinking and exhaustion. If the head of the household has thus collapsed, a wife or daughter of his may make her way to an unmarried visitor's bed and spend part of the night with him.

The next day may be characterized by a "hangover" which is social as well as biochemical, when the various participants, embarrassed or angered over the previous night's events, face each other in the plain light of day. Hurried leave-takings may occur as visitors depart for their homes. While the early part of the prior evening's party may have given rise to temporary feelings of good fellowship, the later activities commonly tend to result in a "morning after" whose brooding mood hardly gives the impression that the parties are a clear-cut mechanism for social solidarity.

The most successful party-givers and hosts are those men who, in addition to having two or three wives to produce large amounts of beer and food, are respected by their neighbors for: their renown as killers in feuds and war, or as shamans; the achievement of age sufficient to have grandchildren; and who are generally of an amiable, honest, and magnanimous nature when dealing with those who are not their enemies. A man who has most of these characteristics is referred to by the term *untä*, which means "big" or "old" man. The demeanor of party participants in the house of such a man tends to be more circumspect and respectful of the master of the house, and excesses such as arguments and brawls seem to occur less often.

While the concept of the *untä* ideally encompasses all of the characteristics described, it is possible to acquire the designation with no formal qualifications other than simply having lived long enough to exhibit a few gray hairs and to have many grandchildren. Such an achievement receives respect as a sign of supernatural power, and an elderly *untä* of this sort is believed to have the ability to curse to death anyone who incurs his anger. No other kind of person is considered to possess this ability. Partly out of fear of being cursed, young men in the neighborhood assist him in land clearing and other tasks when he requests their aid. While the elderly *untä*'s opinion is normally respected, he usually is not a real leader unless he is also outstanding as a killer, shaman, or good host. Thus the true "big men" are distinguished not only by longevity but by real leadership and generosity.

Kakaram, *the "Powerful Ones"*

Given such factors as the absence of any formal political organization and even of unilineal descent groups, as well as the pervasive belief in shamanistically induced illness and death, the conflict over women, and the emphasis on retaliatory sanctions and feuding, it should not be unexpected that the leaders in Jívaro society are outstanding killers and shamans. Although such leadership is informal, almost all neighborhoods have at least one or two noted killers and a few superior shamans who are valued as protectors of their neighboring relatives, or at least of those with whom they are on friendly terms. Such leadership roles are earned and, in the case of the killers, acquired literally through life-and-death struggle.

The outstanding killer gains prestige and social obligations by helping the people of his locality in eliminating their enemies. Such a man is known as *kakaram* ("powerful" or "powerful one") and also, if he is not too youthful, as *untä*. He is believed to possess an unusually large quantity of *arutam* soul power (see pp. 135–43) (*kakarma*), which both protects him from death and is believed to drive him on to kill as often as possible.[3]

The majority of young men interviewed expressed a strong desire to kill, not only to avenge the deaths of their fathers and other close relatives, but to acquire the *arutam* soul power and to become known, respected, and feared as *kakaram*. To be acknowledged as a *kakaram*, a man must have killed at least several persons. Early in his career, he does this by going on killing expeditions led by others, whether intra-tribal assassinations or the inter-tribal raids for *tsantsa*. As his reputation increases, he will eventually successfully organize and lead such an expedition himself, usually the more modest local assassination raid, probably against a specific personal enemy who is believed to have, sometime earlier, caused the death of a member of his immediate family. If he acquits himself well in achieving this assassination, especially as evidenced by firing the first shot into the victim, word will rapidly spread of his apparent power. Soon he will be approached by other men to lead them in killing expeditions against their own enemies. The *kakaram*, anxious to further his reputation as well as to gain additional supernatural power through more killing, rarely refuses such a request, even though it often means that he is agreeing to kill a fellow tribesman who is not even an enemy of his.

As his reputation grows, the *kakaram* tends to dress himself in elaborate feather headdresses and ornaments when visiting other households or receiving guests (see frontispiece). Similarly, he adopts an ever more forceful and aggressive style of speaking when receiving visitors, meeting others on the trail, or in visiting other men. He conveys the impression of being invincible in every aspect of his public demeanor. If he has a son, he encourages him to become a killer also, and instructs him to the extent of taking him on assassination expeditions even as early as the age of six or seven years. Although such a young boy will not yet take part in the actual killing, the father brings him up to the corpse after the murder and has him fire into it, with the father helping him hold the gun. The wives of such a *kakaram* also are expected to outperform other women in making superior pottery vessels, doing garden work and other aspects of household labor. Informants said that one way of looking at this was that since a *kakaram* is very much a man, his wives have to be very much women.

While a *kakaram* is greatly feared by his enemies, his neighbors usually look upon him as a great local asset, a deterrent to attacks upon them, and refer to him with the title *untä* (big) before his name, especially if he is also hospitable to them and generous with beer and food. Of course, there may be neighbors who get into a quarrel or other dispute with him; but they almost always move as soon as possible to another region of the tribe where they feel more secure. Thus there is a continual process of self-selection in terms of the composition of any neighborhood, which tends to reduce local antagonisms.

When a *kakaram* has become really famous, even his worst personal enemies may come to him to ask for help in killing someone. To make such a request, an enemy, accompanied by at least one bodyguard, will approach the house of the *kakaram*, firing his gun several times and frequently giving the standard visitor's yell, so that it will be clear that they are not on a hostile mission of stealth. Upon arriving at the house, the visiting enemy is offered beer and food, in keeping with Jívaro etiquette. The host is also honor-bound not to attack anyone visiting him peaceably, at least while the visitor is in the house and its environs. However, secret poisoning of proffered beer is assumed to be common, and the enemy may decline to drink, even though the woman serving it dips her hand into the bowl and sucks it to show that the beer is safe, a standard demonstration in serving all visitors. It is more likely, though, that he will accept the beer to demonstrate his confidence in his own invulnerability.

To avoid having the women or anyone else other than the *kakaram* learn the identity of the intended victim, the visitor pulls his stool close to that of the host and converses in whispers. In his conversation, the visitor acknowledges that he is an enemy of the host, and justifies his request not on the basis of any personal weakness or inadequacy, but because of the need for additional manpower in the expedition. If the *kakaram* has no reservations about killing the particular person discussed, he will almost always accept the invitation to kill. Partially this is due to general factors such as his desire to accumulate *arutam* soul power through killing and to further his prestige, but in this particular kind of situation, his acceptance is also due to his reluctance to lose face with his enemy. A refusal to participate probably would be interpreted as weakness or fear, unless he could give an acceptable excuse in terms of a kinship or friendship bond with the intended victim.

The Jívaro recognize that one of the major motivations for asking a *kakaram* who is an enemy for killing assistance is the hope to shoot him in the back while on the trail. Therefore, if he agrees to participate in a killing expedition with his enemy, he takes the precaution of bringing along at least one trustworthy close relative, such as a brother, for the express purpose of "covering" him. A *kakaram*, since he believes himself to be invulnerable to death (see pp. 135–43), does this primarily so that he will not be wounded. While the "buddy" system of protection tends to work fairly well in daylight, there still is a danger that the *kakaram* may be shot at night, when his partner cannot see who attacked him.

After the successful completion of the killing expedition, and if there has been no untoward incident, all the participants return to the *kakaram*'s house, since, according to custom, all killing parties have as their point of departure and return the house of the leader. There he will formally point out to those who invited him that although they are his enemies, he has helped them kill someone who was an enemy of theirs. He asks them if they want him to continue being their enemy or whether they would prefer to live in peace. Invariably the inviters reply that they, too, wish to start living in peace. However, this tends to be essentially a stereotypical ritual with little or no binding effect. Feuding normally soon resumes as before.

A *kakaram* is also often invited to lead killing expeditions by persons who are not his enemies, from both his own and other neighborhoods. These invitations provide him with an opportunity to build alliances, since non-enemies who invite him have a recognized reciprocal obligation to assist him in an assassination or war raid if he should request it. Thus, if a man leads many expeditions and thereby becomes a *ti kakaram* ("very powerful one"), he may theoretically have on call almost all the men of several neighborhoods and some of the men of a number of other localities. However, such alliances are quite unstable, and the men's response to a particular request will be very much conditioned by their evaluations of the immediate situation in terms of their own self-interest. By the time a *ti kakaram* is achieving such status and power, he tends to be already elderly, and, instead of continuing to lead expeditions himself, will usually send his sons or sons-in-law.

A famous *kakaram* sometimes may even be sent an invitation, through intermediaries, to kill someone in another tribe, usually an Achuara. The invitation sent by the non-Jívaro carries with it the tacit understanding that the *kakaram* and his followers, since they are from another tribe, will conduct themselves in the form of a war raid, rather than the intra-tribal assassination expedition which goes after only a single victim. Thus they are expected to attack the entire household of the intended victim, taking heads and seizing women. The inviter is usually someone with great hatred for his enemy who views the bringing in of outsiders to do the job as an opportunity for retribution beyond anything that he could do directly. He will guide the *kakaram* and his war party to the house of the victim and, after the attack, one of the grateful head-takers will give their guide a shotgun as a token of appreciation.

The co-operation provided by such non-*untsuri šuarä* inviters has sometimes made it possible for the Jívaro to travel incredibly far to kill. In one fondly remembered case, the assistance given by a *tsumu šuarä* (Huambisa) inviter-guide made it possible for a Jívaro expedition to pass down the Río Santiago by canoe through the entire Huambisa tribe and to wipe out most of an Aguaruna household on the Río Marañon below the Pongo de Manseriche.

Shamans and Shaman Hierarchies

Shamans (*uwišin*), more numerous than outstanding killers, often wield considerable power in the neighborhood. The bewitching shamans (*wawek*, or *yahauči uwišin:* bad shaman) derive their social influence primarily from the fear in which they are held by their neighbors. Their mildly expressed wishes are often interpreted as near commands by laymen. The curing type of shaman (*peŋer uwišin:* good shaman) exercises a less ominous type of social power, deriving primarily from the fact that his neighbors tend to view him as an important asset to their welfare. They normally court his favor in order to assure themselves of his future willingness to cure them or members of their family.

In terms of material goods, shamans are invariably the wealthiest persons and usually candidly admit that they supply their services primarily for the purpose of gaining valuables. They expect to be paid for their curing or bewitching services with the most highly valued goods available. A single treatment normally nets a curing shaman at least a muzzle-loading shotgun, for example. Often a blowgun, a hunting dog, or a machete is thrown in. Curers often refuse to visit a distant patient unless paid in advance, and, even then, may demand additional payment if the cure requires more than a single night's ministrations.

Among the Jívaro, a request for a gift cannot be refused without the denier "losing face," making it difficult for the majority of persons to hoard quantities of possessions. While non-shamans continually badger each other for gifts, thereby preventing the accumulation of wealth by a few individuals among themselves, they almost never ask shamans for goods, fearing the wrath of the bewitchers and wishing to cultivate the goodwill of the curers. Thus shamans are usually the only persons able to accumulate significant quantities of goods.

Shamans frequently utilize their wealth and social influence to secure specific services from their non-shaman neighbors.

Several cases were encountered in which men gave their daughters in marriage to shamans without the customary bride-service, or even the less common bride-price, because the girls' fathers feared the bewitching power of the shamans. It is also standard practice for shamans to be given gifts of chickens, clothing, and ornaments during casual visits to laymen's houses, even though the shamans have not specifically asked for them. Laymen, in contrast, are usually not given presents by fellow non-shamans without asking for them. Shamans are quite conscious of their privileges, and often boasted to me how well they (compared to non-shamans) were fed when visiting neighbors' houses.

Shamans host neighbors to help in land clearing more often than do non-shamans. Such labor is ostensibly reciprocal, but the shaman's neighbors are reluctant to ask him to work for them in turn. This is partly due to their desire to maintain his goodwill, but there also seems to be a feeling that extensive manual labor is not in keeping with the shaman's supernatural preoccupations and services.

A shaman obtains his power to bewitch or cure exclusively through purchase. To become a shaman, a man presents a sizeable gift to an established practitioner. Such a gift must have some real value in native terms. Typically, it consists of one or two muzzle-loading shotguns, gunpowder, shot, primers, a blowgun and curare, and a machete or steel axehead. In return for this payment, the practicing shaman instructs the apprentice in his new profession and supplies him with magical power, in the form of the spirit servants called *tsentsak* (see pp. 154–66). The exchange of shamanistic power for payment in material valuables (*kuit*) makes the two men *amigri* or "friends," as is the case with normal trading partners (see pp. 128–31). However, the relationship between shamans is a hierarchical one significantly different from the essentially egalitarian one between ordinary *amigri*.

The essence of the shaman's power, the *tsentsak*, or magical darts, have an almost infinite variety of forms, and are viewed as invisible spirit helpers which normally reside in the shaman's body. To bewitch, the shaman sends one of these invisible darts into the body of his victim. To cure, he calls upon these spirit aides to suck the intruding magical dart out of the patient's body.

The power of the magical darts is believed to vary according to their type and according to the power of the shaman supplying them. The most powerful, and therefore most valued, supernatural darts are considered to be those belonging to the shamans of the Quichua (Quechua)-speaking Canelos tribe, which extends northward from the Jívaro to the headwaters of the Río Napo. The Canelos tribe has long been in contact with missionaries, and Canelos shamans are distinguished by the Jívaro with a separate term, *payü*, derived from *banco*, the Spanish word for the "bank" part of a placer-mining apparatus, which retains the gold-bearing gravels. Canelos shamans call themselves "banks" because they are believed to be similar rich repositories, but of magical power instead of mineral wealth.

The Canelos *payü* are said to possess "white man's" *tsentsak*, which the Jívaro and Achuara shamans consider superior to their own traditional *šuar*, or Indian, *tsentsak*. By means of "white man's" magical darts, the Canelos shamans are able to perform feats not possible for Jívaro and Achuara shamans. For example, they are the only shamans in the region who are able to become possessed with the souls of the dead and to act as oral mediums. They also, it is believed, can send demons to possess victims and thereby manipulate their behavior. Furthermore, these Canelos shamans are so powerful that it is assumed that they cannot be killed by ordinary means.

The Jívaro and Achuara believe so strongly in the superiority of the Canelos *payü* that men wishing to become successful shamans would prefer to obtain their own supernatural darts directly from them. A man cannot expect to become a successful shaman, either in bewitching or curing, unless he has magical darts which exceed in power those of the shamans against whom he is working. Beyond this, he believes that his very survival will depend upon the ability of his own magical darts or spirit helpers to resist the attacks of their counterparts belonging to enemy shamans.

The intensity of feuding within the Jívaro and Achuara tribes makes long-distance travel to obtain *tsentsak* too dangerous to be undertaken by most men. Generally, only the most northern of the Jívaro and Achuara shamans succeed in visiting the Canelos *payü* in order to obtain power. For this reason, the northern Jívaro and Achuara shamans are considered to be more powerful than those to the south.

Since shamanistic power declines in its strength as it is passed southward from shaman to shaman, a southern member of these two tribes who wishes to acquire superior shamanistic power simply does the best he can—which is to travel as far north as safety permits to obtain his magical darts. This is rarely more than forty to fifty miles. If the pilgrim is relatively fortunate, he may be able to get his power from a shaman who has obtained his darts directly from a Canelos bank. But if he lives farther south, he may find he can only obtain the darts from a shaman who got them from a shaman who got them from a shaman who got them from a *payü!* Thus, among the Jívaro and the Achuara, there is a regular traffic of shamans making pilgrimages at least slightly northward from their neighborhoods to secure strong supernatural power.

Upon returning home, a shaman soon barters part of his power, in turn, to men coming to visit him from the south, or he may also dispense it to men of his own neighborhood who are unwilling to undertake even the short trip northward. In any event, the shaman may directly supply power to no more than four men. After that, his power is believed to be so drained off that he must obtain a new supply of magical darts.

The relationship between the shaman supplying the magical power and the person receiving it is not a relationship between equals. The power-giver is referred to in these tribes as the "higher" shaman, and the recipient as the "lower." The "higher" and "lower" designations refer to actual authority and control exercised by the giver of power over the recipient. The higher shaman, it is believed, can magically take back the power which he has conferred, regardless of the distance separating the two shamans (see pp. 165–66). He may take back this power because of a personal offense, or because he has been bribed to do so by an enemy of the lower shaman. Such occurrences are frequently reported, and there are a number of former shamans who testify that they lost their power in this manner.

A sudden loss of shamanistic power is believed to result in serious illness and often in death. The lower shaman, therefore, tends to fear his higher associate and attempts to keep on good terms with him. With this purpose in mind, he sends tribute in the form of substantial gifts of material valuables (*kuit*) at regular intervals. Such *kuit* includes shotguns, hunting dogs, blowguns, curare, feather headbands (*tawaspä*), and Western-manufactured shirts and trousers. He particularly hopes that these gifts will offset any bribes that may be offered to the higher shaman.

A secondary incentive for sending tribute is the need of the lower shaman to replenish his supply of magical darts every few years. His power, in the form of these spirit servants, is gradually used up through curing, bewitching, or dispensing it. He expects, therefore, to have to replenish his supply by visiting his higher associate. The lower shaman may look forward to help from the higher man only if he has been faithful in the submission of goods.

Tribute between shamans flows from the south, since, of course, the most powerful shamans are in the north. The tribute follows the lines of the shaman hierarchies up into the Canelos tribe. These hierarchies do not converge upon a single Canelos shaman, however, because there are a number of banks of about equal power in the tribe. In other words, this is basically a system of plural and parallel hierarchies culminating in the same region, but not in the same individual.

The hierarchical situation is further complicated by the fact that a given shaman frequently obtains magical power from several higher associates. He does this so that his power cannot be completely taken away from him at the whim of a single higher shaman. This tendency seems to prevent the hierarchies from being used as chains of authority. Since a shaman is thus often directly subordinate to several others, considerable intertwining of hierarchical relationships occurs (see Figure 3).

Roughly speaking, about one out of every four adult men is a shaman, so that, in any given locality, the shamans constitute a significant proportion of the male population. A few women are shamans, but among the Jívaro this is basically a man's occupation. The shamans in any particular neighborhood are ordinarily linked together by secret partnerships. These partnerships are also hierarchical in nature, and often a single shaman is the formally recognized leader of all the shamans in a specific neighborhood. These secret

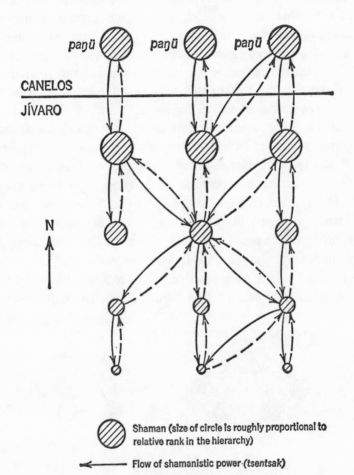

FIGURE 3

Schematic diagram of inter-tribal shamanistic hierarchies

partnerships often link together four or five or more shamans in the same neighborhood, the higher partner supplying *tsentsak*, and his lower partners reciprocating with native and Western trade goods (*kuit*). Since bewitchers can create only bewitchers, while curers can create both bewitchers and curers (see pp. 155–56), the local hierarchies tend to have the forms shown in Figure 4.

Ex-shamans have testified that intra-neighborhood shaman partners who are bewitchers sometimes even go to the length of mildly bewitching disliked neighbors so that their curing shaman partners can profit in trade goods from treating the induced illness. The bewitching partner expects his curing shaman associate, in turn, never to tell a layman that the former was responsible for an illness or death. The curing shaman may even give his bewitching partner an occasional gift from his accumulated store of wealth, thus reversing the usual flow of *kuit* (see Figure 4, B). More frequently,

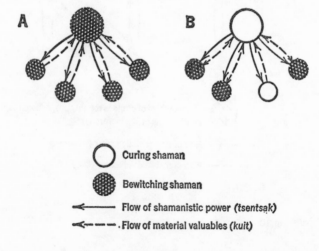

    ◯   Curing shaman

    ⬤   Bewitching shaman

    ◄——— Flow of shamanistic power (*tsentsak*)

    ◄— — — Flow of material valuables (*kuit*)

FIGURE 4

Schematic diagram of local shamanistic hierarchies

the curing shaman covertly reciprocates by later supplying his bewitching partner with a new supply of supernatural power in exchange for only a minor payment, instead of the normally major gift of a shotgun.

A local bewitching shaman hierarchy also sometimes acts in concert as a "raiding party" to go together to kill, through witchcraft, a common enemy in another neighborhood. Using the method indicated elsewhere (see pp. 157–58), they secretly shoot their *tsentsak* from hiding near the house of their intended victim and then return home. Frequently, they remain together a few days in the house of their higher partner to await word that the enemy has become ill. Informants claimed that such concerted action "always" resulted in the intended victim immediately becoming ill.

Trading Partners

With conflict and violence common, and lacking any corporate kinship groups to provide security, the Jívaro create social bonds by making "friends" (*amigri*) in a formalized manner through the exchange of trade goods. Such *amigri* pairs, or trading partnerships, constitute the strongest male social units within the same generation. These partners become mutually obligated to one another to a degree exceeding the obligations of brothers. In fact, it is not unusual for brothers, or even fathers and sons, to become "friends" in order to formalize their sense of mutual obligation to one another. While trading partners commonly live in different neighborhoods, many *amigri* dwell in the same neighborhood, and sometimes even in the same house. Households within the same neighborhood, linked by such formalized bonds, tend to have a higher degree of unity than is normally the case.

The relationship between a trading partner and his neighbors who are not his formal *amigri* is a key aspect of the system. A man becomes an *amigri* not to accumulate and hoard wealth, but to dispense it in his neighborhood, to gain prestige and obligations. The distribution of these goods locally is normally done piecemeal as the trading partner's relatives and others ask him for them. Informants, in saying that a man becomes an *amigri* "so that people will like him," explicitly recognize that the main purpose of being a trading partner, and of distributing the goods obtained thereby, is to acquire friends. The people who receive goods from a partner become morally obligated to him until they reciprocate with either an equivalent amount of goods or with services, the latter usually in the form of aid in the trading partner's social disputes and feuds. The *amigri* is usually far from upset if his neighbors do not repay him immediately, for the longer they delay in repayment, the longer period of time they are obligated to him. A trading partner is also likely to be aided by his neighbors in disputes for the additional reason that they wish to protect their future source of supply of trade goods. Altogether, although the usual trading partner is not a community leader, he obtains an above average degree of social security in a society where security is not easily obtained, by exchanging trade goods for friendship and obligations.

These native traders are the chief means whereby the interior Jívaro have acquired significant quantities of machetes, steel axes, and firearms from the frontier of Ecuadorian colonization west of the Cordillera de Cutucú. Chains of native traders also connect the interior Jívaro with the Canelos tribe to the north and with the Achuara Jivaroans to the east and southeast. In its total extent, this network of Indian trading partners apparently stretches from the foot of the Andes in the west to near Iquitos on the Amazon in the east, and from the Río Napo in the north to the Río Marañon in the south. Its most complex and intensive manifestations occur in the isolated interior, where the native distribution system is uninterrupted by white traders or colonization.

Trade in the interior involves two kinds of commodities about equally: white-manufactured valuables (*apačï kuit*) and Indian-manufactured valuables (*šuar kuit*), the latter particularly from the Achuara tribe. The frontier Jívaro west of the Cutucú mountain range, who are in direct contact with the whites at Macas, Sucúa, and other smaller settlements, obtain the Western-manufactured items primarily by engaging in wage labor for the whites. These then are carried over the Cutucú range by means of several different foot trails.

The Achuara people to the east, lacking any such direct source of large quantities of steel cutting tools and guns, have to trade with the interior Jívaro to obtain them. The Achuara, for their part, have a near monopoly on the manufacture of blowguns and curare, and produce feather ornaments which are highly esteemed by the Jívaro. The Achuara also supply various monkeys, parrots, and marmosets, as well as such items as woven kilts, ornamental earsticks, and native beadwork. In addition, they are the sole suppliers of glass beads, which, for an unknown reason, are available in the Peruvian Amazon, but not in the Ecuadorian Oriente. Except for these glass beads and some .44 caliber cartridges, Achuara trade in items from Peru is severely limited, apparently because the only native-produced goods in which the Peruvians are interested are jaguar, ocelot, and especially peccary hides. The geographical isolation of the Achuara

rules out the possibility of their obtaining Western-manufactured goods by entering into any labor relationship with
whites.

The Achuara also rely upon the Jívaro to supply them
with much of their salt. The Achuara have access to a distant
rock salt deposit of inferior quality on the Río Marañon
far to the south in Peru, but prefer to trade with the Jívaro
to secure the purer salt evaporated from two springs in
the Cordillera de Cutucú, one near the upper Río Mangosiza and the other near the Río Yaupi (see Map 2 and
Plate 18).

This system of native traders is composed of pairs of
men normally living one to two days' walk apart who visit
each other every two and a half to four months. The visiting trading partner, if he comes from the west, i.e., from
the white-Jívaro frontier, brings machetes, steel axes, and
shotguns. If from the east, he primarily carries Achuara-
made products.

These pairs of men, or trading partners, formalize their
essentially contractual relationship with a ritual and thereafter address one another in the diminutive as "little friend,"
i.e., *amiči*. While the term *amigri* is the third person possessive
form of *amigü*, from the Spanish word *amigo*, the development and meaning of the relationship is distinctly native.[4]
Two men normally decide to become "friends" only after
a series of informal visits, during which they may have
exchanged small gifts. When they agree to enter into the
formalized trading partnership, each spends two or more
months collecting goods that are scarce in his future partner's
neighborhood. Then one visits the house of the other; a
cloth is spread on the dirt floor and the gifts of both parties
are placed in two piles on the cloth. Each man kneels

beside his pile facing the other. Each says, "Take these things," and they embrace. The two men's wives then go through the same ritual, and finally, both men and their wives all embrace each other.

In this first exchange of goods between *amigri*, and also in subsequent exchanges, usually several large baskets of goods are involved. A typical inventory of goods given by the man coming from the east consists of feather ornaments, beads, blowguns, blowgun dart poison, a hunting dog, and a home-woven kilt. The other man, with white man's goods from the west, presents black powder, shot, percussion caps, a machete, knives, and a shotgun.

Following the first exchange, the host says to the other, "I will bring you valuables (*kuit*). You do the same for me." His visitor in turn, says, "When I send word to you, then you come to visit me." Such word, when it is transmitted later, usually is carried by some other visitor between the neighborhoods of the two *amigri*. When the former host (often accompanied by a wife) returns the visit, he receives a most hospitable reception. In fact, trading partners tend to try to outdo one another in their generosity. If one man fed the other much chicken during his earlier visit, his friend may then feel it necessary to kill a pig to supply his guest with even a greater quantity of choice meat. If he has no pig to kill, then at least he insists that his guest and his wife take half of the household's chickens back with them when they return home. The giving of half of one's easily transportable valuables to one's *amigri* is a characteristic feature of the trading partnership.

Amigri are expected to exchange equal amounts of goods with each other, at least over a period of several months, if not in a single transaction. There are standard recognized barter "prices" which guide them in this. In the interior region, typical equivalences in trade goods are the following:

Trade Goods from the West	EQUALS	Trade Goods from the East (*Achuara*)
1 pot of salt		1 blowgun
1 pot of salt		1 gourd of blowgun dart poison
1 machete or 1 steel axe-head		1 blowgun
1 single-barrelled muzzle-loading shotgun		1 red toucan feather headband (*tawaspä*)

The precise equivalences of trade goods in the interior region, of course, are not the same as in other parts of the Jívaro territory because of regional differences in the scarcity of various kinds of goods. For example, west of the Cordillera de Cutucú in the frontier zone, the greater quantity of Western-manufactured goods and the lesser supply of Achuara-manufactured goods raises the "prices" which must be paid in the former for the latter.

In actual practice, trading partners do not keep a strict accounting of transactions. Since a variety of valuables is exchanged by two "friends" at one time and since the Jívaro do not value numeration, the exchange is often slightly uneven. In terms of Jivaroan morality, however, it is apparently unthinkable that a "friend" would consistently attempt to take advantage of his partner in such transactions. To do so would jeopardize the continuance of the *amigri* relationship, and possibly the obligation of the host partner to protect the life of his partner against any local enemies.

The *amigri* relationship is viewed as being closer than that of siblings and, in fact, if two brothers happen to be trading partners they will use the "friend" form of address (*amiči*) in preference to that normally used by brothers (*yatsuči*). Brothers, fathers, and sons can and often do fight with one another, but it seems to be unthinkable for a man to fight with his "friend." A man is born and married into his personal kindred and it is recognized that he does not necessarily have to like his relatives, but in the case of a trading partner, he is honor-bound to live up to the obligation which he has ritually undertaken. If he failed to do so, he would lose the respect and trust of others to a degree dangerous to his safety.

The protection of a visiting "friend" by his host-partner involves constant companionship as a bodyguard and if possible, even concealment of the identity of his visitor. Thus, when a local neighbor happens to drop in while a trading partner's *amigri* is visiting and asks the name of the visitor, the host-partner may simply state, "He is my friend," and thereby avoid giving any additional information, because his partner might have enemies in the local neighborhood. Such a statement is also a declaration that the visitor, being classified as a "friend," is under the host's personal protection.

The safe conduct provided by his *amigri* is absolutely essential when a Jívaro goes to an Achuara neighborhood to trade, because anyone of the alien tribe has a theoretical right to kill him to obtain his head for a trophy. Without the *amigri* institution, well-developed Jívaro-Achuara trade would be impossible. Even with the safe conduct provided by a trading partner, *amigri* are afraid to travel much farther than one or two days' walk. The longer they are on the trail traveling alone and unprotected to visit a partner, the

greater the chance of being murdered by an enemy. Therefore, a series of trading partners is necessary to transport
goods across the territory of the Jívaro tribe from the frontier
of white colonization to the Achuara and back.

In the Río Cangaimi neighborhood in 1956–57, an *amigri*
named Hintač was the participant in a chain of trading partners extending to near Iquitos, Peru (see Figure 5). His case
provides an example of one such series of trading partners.
He was trading white-manufactured goods and Jívaro salt to
his "friend" Tiwi, an Achuara residing on the lower Río
Macuma. Tiwi, in turn, exchanged goods with his Achuara
amigri, Mukučam, of the *yaŋuntsa* neighborhood. The latter
continued the trade farther to the southeast with Aŋuašä, in
the *čaŋuap* neighborhood. Finally, Aŋuašä then exchanged
goods with a white trader (name unknown) who was reported to live in or near Iquitos.

In the other direction, west from the Río Cangaimi neighborhood, Hintač was a link in another series of trading partners. At the time, he was on extremely hostile terms with
many of the Río Cusuimi people and lacked a "friend" there
for his trade to the west. Consequently, he became an *amigri*
of a man of his own neighborhood who himself had a trading
partner, Kašinhint, in the Cusuimi region, and thereby was
able to effect a continuation of trade westward. Kašinhint, in
turn, traded with Wampútsurek west of the Cordillera de
Cutucú, about half a day's walk from the white settlement
of Sucúa in the Río Upano Valley. Wampútsurek obtained
steel cutting tools, guns, and ammunition for the return trade
primarily from people of his neighborhood who were working for the Ecuadorian colonists in Sucúa.

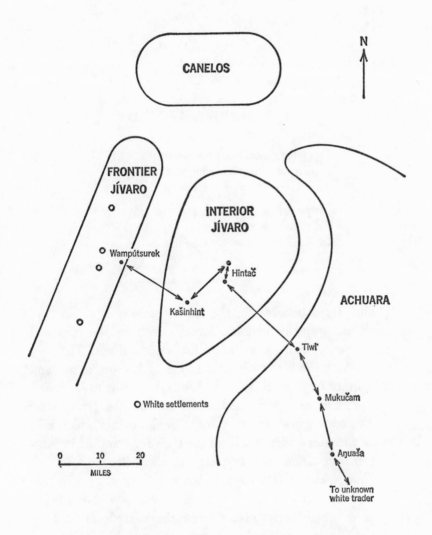

FIGURE 5
Schematic diagram of a trading partnership chain

Chapter IV

THE HIDDEN WORLD

I go where there is a great waterfall.
It emerges where the mountains become stone.
This waterfall will give me strength.

I hope that with this long journey
I shall have an encounter
In order to have a very long life.

From the song of a man making the
trip to encounter an *arutam*

The Jívaro believe that the true determinants of life and death are normally invisible forces which can be seen and utilized only with the aid of hallucinogenic drugs. The normal waking life is explicitly viewed as "false" or "a lie," and it is firmly believed that truth about causality is to be found by entering the supernatural world or what the Jívaro view as the "real" world, for they feel that the events which take place within it underlie and are the basis for many of the surface manifestations and mysteries of daily life.

Thus, within a few days of birth, a baby is given a hallucinogenic drug to help it enter the "real" world and hopefully to obtain help in surviving the hazards of infancy through seeing an "ancient specter." If an older child misbehaves, his parents may administer another, stronger, hallucinogen to enable him to see that the "reality" on which they base their knowledge and authority does indeed exist. Even hunting dogs are given their own special hallucinogen to provide them with the essential contact with the supernatural plane. Finally, entrance into the normally invisible realm is considered so essential to success that the two kinds of leaders in Jívaro society, the outstanding killers (*kakaram*) and shamans, are the two types of persons for whom hallucinogenic drugs tend to have the most important role. Their achievements are believed by the Jívaro to be directly connected to their ability to enter, and utilize the souls and spirits of, that "real" world.

Three kinds of souls are recognized. Of these, the *arutam wakaní* is believed by the Jívaro to be the most significant. This is an acquired soul, and a man may possess as many as two *arutam* souls at one time. The second type of soul is the *muisak*, or avenging soul, while the third is the *nekás wakaní*, the "true," "real," or "ordinary" soul.

The Arutam *Soul*[1]

Arutam wakaní is perhaps best referred to as the "ancient specter" soul. The term *arutam* alone refers to a particular kind of vision or apparition. *Wakaní* alone simply means "soul" or "spirit." Thus the *arutam wakaní* is the particular kind of soul that produces the *arutam*, or vision. An *arutam* appears only occasionally and, when it does, is only in existence for less than a minute. The *arutam* soul, on the other hand, exists eternally once it has been created. It is in the system of thought regarding the *arutam* soul that the Jívaro seek security from the ever felt menace of death.

The Jívaro believe that the possessor of a single *arutam* soul cannot be killed by any form of physical violence, poison, or by sorcery, although he is not immune to death from contagious diseases such as measles and smallpox. In other words, a person who has only one *arutam* soul in his possession is relieved from daily anxiety about being murdered. A Jívaro who is fortunate enough to possess two *arutam* souls cannot die of *any* cause whatever, including contagious disease.

A person is not born with an *arutam* soul. Such a soul must be acquired, and in certain traditional ways. The acquisition of this type of soul is considered to be so important to an adult male's survival that a boy's parents do not expect him to live past puberty without one. Women sometimes obtain *arutam* souls, but it is not considered so essential for them. One reason is that intra-tribal killing, the most common source of violent death, is primarily directed at adult males rather than at women and children.

A boy begins seeking an *arutam* soul at about the age of six years. Accompanied most commonly by his father, he makes a pilgrimage to the sacred waterfall in his neighborhood. This is always the highest waterfall within a few days' travel. It is believed to be the rendezvous of these souls or spirits which wander about as breezes, scattering the spray of the long cascade. During the day, the vision seekers "bathe" in the waterfall by striding back and forth under its cold and drenching canopy, actually walking between the downpour and the cliff from which it is dropping. They walk naked and shivering, and in some danger from falling logs which may be swept over the cliff with the current. Each paces with the aid of a magical balsa wood staff carved for the occasion, and chants, "*tau, tau, tau,*" continually. By night the pilgrims sleep near the falls in a simple lean-to. Here they fast, drink tobacco water (made by steeping green tobacco leaves in cold water), and await the appearance of an *arutam.*

They may keep up this fasting, "bathing," and tobacco water drinking for as long as five days. If unsuccessful, they return home to make another attempt at a later date. More likely, though, is that before the five days are up, one of the members of the party will have recourse to drinking hallucinogenic *maikua* (*Datura arborea*) juice. Usually this is a person who has failed to see an *arutam* on a previous vision quest or who feels an urgent need to see one without delay.

Maikua, of which the Jívaro distinguish and use six different types, is recognized by them to be the most powerful and also the most dangerous hallucinogen with which they are familiar. In their pharmacopoeia, the hallucinogenic plants with which they are acquainted are ranked thusly in terms of their strength: (1) all six forms of *maikua*; (2) *natemä*, mixed with *yahi* (see pp. 153–54), and *parápara*; (3) *tsentsemä*, *pirípiri*, and *típuru*. The last four remain to be botanically identified with certainty.

The psychotropic potency of *Datura* and certain other plants of the Solanaceae is well known to Western pharmacology, their hallucinogenic properties being due primarily to their high content of hyoscyamine, atropine, and scopolamine.[2] Preparations from these plants tend to produce, in large dosages, a state of excitation, delirium, and hallucinations, followed by a state of narcosis.[3]

The Jívaro obtain their hallucinatory experiences with *Datura* by ingesting the raw juice of the green bark of the stems. The effects begin to be felt within about three to four minutes of ingestion, probably because of the fast action of the atropine. The *arutam* seeker ingesting the *Datura* juice is never supposed to do it without the presence of an adult who is not taking the drug. It is the responsibility of the latter to provide psychological support or, in Jívaro terms, to "encourage" him, and also to hold him down, if necessary, during the first phase of the intoxication, when the drug taker tends to become delirious and is in danger of running off into the forest in his highly agitated state and, as a result, possibly falling off a cliff or into a river and drowning. The other pilgrims in the party do not take the substance themselves, partially so that they can protect the *maikua* drinker from running off. They also believe that an *arutam* is not likely to come to a vision seeker if he is a coward, which would be evidenced if he were unwilling to take *Datura* alone and enter the normally invisible world unaccompanied.

If the *arutam* seeker is fortunate, he will awaken at about midnight to find the stars gone from the sky, the earth trembling, and a great wind felling the trees of the forest amid thunder and lightning. To keep from being blown down, he grasps a tree trunk and awaits the *arutam*. Shortly the *arutam* appears from the depths of the forest, often in the form of a pair of large creatures. The particular animal forms can vary considerably, but some of the most common *arutam* include a pair of giant jaguars fighting one another as they roll over and over towards the vision seeker, or two anacondas doing the same. Often the vision may simply be a single huge disembodied human head or a ball of fire drifting through the forest towards the *arutam* seeker. When the apparition arrives to within twenty or thirty feet, the Jívaro must run forward and touch it, either with a small stick or his hand. This is said to require a good deal of courage, and sometimes the person flees the *arutam* instead. But if he does run forward and touch the vision, it instantly explodes like dynamite and disappears.[4]

Upon thus achieving success in encountering an *arutam*, the person returns to his house, but tells no one that he has accomplished the purpose of his quest. Arriving home, he goes alone to sleep that night on the bank of the nearest river. After nightfall, the soul of the same *arutam* he touched comes to him as he dreams. His dream visitor is in the form of an old Jívaro man who says to him, "I am your ancestor. Just as I have lived a long time, so will you. Just as I have

12. Man wearing an *etsemat* (woven cotton band with toucan feather tassels), the most common traditional head garb (Río Cangaimi, 1956–57).

13. Profile of the same individual.

14. Man with *etsemat* and ear sticks. His face painting, of achiote, is purely for beautification. The shirt was obtained through the native trading partnership system (Río Cangaimi, 1956–57).

15. Profile of same individual, showing native comb holding his hair and *etsemat* in place.

16. Visitors to an uncompleted house receiving manioc beer prior to engaging in conversation with the host. Guns are always carried on visits and prominently displayed (Río Cusuimi, 1956–57).

17. Host in typical pose when receiving visitors. Hand is cupped over mouth and shotgun cradled in lap (region between the upper Río Macuma and the upper Río Cangaimi, 1956–57).

18. The saline spring from which almost all of the salt used by the interior Jívaro is obtained. Those living within a day or two of the spring boil the water in pots and trade the resultant salt to more distant neighborhoods (near the upper Río Mangosiza in the eastern Cordillera de Cutucú, 1956–57).

19. Man wearing hair unbound, as is often customary when at home in the absence of visitors (Río Cangaimi, 1956–57).

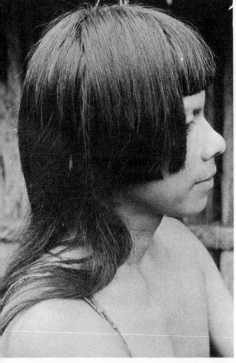

20. Profile of the same individual.

21. Three excellent examples of *tsantsa* (shrunken head trophies). The long cotton strings dangling from the mouths are put on only at the time of the third and last *tsantsa* feast (photo courtesy of the American Museum of Natural History).

22. Shaman boiling *Banisteriopsis* vines and leaves to prepare the hallucinogenic drink *natemä* (Río Tutanangoza, 1964).

23. Snake *tsentsak* seen in a patient's body by a shaman under the influence of *natemä*. Drawn by the shaman subsequent to the experience (Río Tutanangoza, 1964).

24. Halo or "crown" over the head of a shaman under the influence of *natemä* as seen by another shaman who has also taken the drug. Drawn subsequent to the experience. (Río Tutanangoza, 1964).

killed many times, so will you." Without another word the old man disappears and immediately the *arutam* soul of this unknown ancestor enters the body of the dreamer, where it is lodged in his chest.

Upon acquiring this *arutam* soul, the person feels a sudden power surge into his body, accompanied by a new self-confidence. The *arutam* soul is supposed to increase a person's power in the most general sense. This power, called *kakarma*, is believed to increase one's intelligence as well as simple physical strength, and also to make it difficult for the soul possessor to lie or commit other dishonorable acts. His newly acquired power increases his resistance to contagious disease to some degree, but most important, it makes it impossible for him to die as a result of any physical violence or sorcery. Most of his relatives and acquaintances shortly know that he has acquired an *arutam* soul simply because of the change in his personality. For example, he especially tends to speak with great forcefulness.[5] However, he must not tell anyone that he has acquired such a soul, or it will desert him.

When one has thus obtained an *arutam* soul, he generally is seized with a tremendous desire to kill, and it is ordinarily only a matter of a few months before he joins a killing expedition. If he is a young boy, he will accompany his father. The rare women who possess *arutam* souls kill primarily by means of poisoning food or manioc beer.

Jívaro killing expeditions usually attack the victim's house just before dawn. Late in the afternoon of the day prior to the attack, the expedition halts in the forest about a quarter of a mile from its intended objective. There, in their concealed location, the participants must "declare" what kind of *arutam* they had each seen. The younger men form a circle around several of the most experienced killers, who then ask each man in turn to describe the *arutam* that he had seen. As each man, young and old, does this, the soul of his *arutam* leaves his body forever, to roam the forest again as a wind, for *arutam* souls "are satisfied with one killing."⁶ The departing *arutam* souls reportedly generate winds, thunder, and lightning. Eventually, at some time in the indefinite future, each soul is expected once more to enter the body of another Jívaro.

The warriors, having made their declarations, are ready to attack the following morning. Although each of them has just lost an *arutam* soul, the power of that soul remains in the body, only ebbing away gradually. The complete loss of this power is generally believed to take about two weeks. Since the power decreases slowly, the members of the killing party still retain enough of it the next morning so that they cannot be killed by the enemy in battle. If one of their number *is* killed in the attack, the other members of the expedition simply consider the death to be evidence that the deceased had already lost his *arutam* soul without realizing it. As soon as the expedition kills its intended victim, all its members again become entitled to obtain the soul of a new *arutam* upon their return home.

Sometimes the attackers fail in their assault on the intended victim's house. When such a failure occurs, the expedition must immediately choose a new victim and go after him at once, usually without returning home. If these men failed to kill someone, they would not be entitled to obtain new *arutam* souls, and without new *arutam* souls, they would expect to die within weeks or, at the most, months. Since it is therefore a matter of life or death to them, the members of the killing party invariably find an enemy, or at least some stranger, to assassinate. When the killing is accomplished, they return home and each immediately seeks to encounter an *arutam* again and thus to get himself a new soul.

The acquisition of such a new *arutam* soul not only brings the new power, or *kakarma*, of the incoming soul but also serves to "lock in" the power of the previous one and thereby prevent it from ebbing away from the body. A person is limited to possession of not more than two *arutam* souls simultaneously, but this "lock-in" feature of the new soul makes it possible for a person to accumulate the *power* of an indefinite number of previous souls. In other words, while the acquisition of the souls is consecutive, the acquisition of the power is cumulative.

By repeatedly killing, one can continually accumulate power through the replacement of old *arutam* souls with new ones. This "trade-in" mechanism is an important feature because, when a person has had the same *arutam* soul for four or five years, it tends to leave its sleeping possessor to wander nightly through the forest. Sooner or later, while it is thus drifting through the trees, another Jívaro will "steal" it. Accordingly, it is highly desirable to obtain a new soul before the old one begins nocturnal wanderings. This felt need encourages the individual to participate in a killing expedition every few years.

Since a man with an *arutam* soul cannot die as the result of physical violence, poisoning, or witchcraft, i.e., any interpersonal attack, a person who wishes to kill a specific enemy attempts to steal his *arutam* soul away from him as a prelude to assassinating him. This soul-stealing or capturing process involves drinking large quantities of an infusion of *natemä*, beating a hollowed-out log signal drum, and repeating the name of the intended victim. Then if the enemy's *arutam* soul is wandering nocturnally, it may one night hear the would-be assassin's call and, "taking pity" on his need for such a soul, enter his body, never to return to the body of its former possessor.[7]

The Jívaro warrior desires to have personally—and thus

definitely—stolen the *arutam* soul of his intended victim. This feat is often not possible, however, and the would-be murderer instead watches for signs coming to him through gossip or direct observation that the enemy already has had his *arutam* soul taken away by someone else. Such signs or indications, for example, would include rumors of physical weakness or illness on the part of the intended victim, or the first-hand observation that the enemy was lacking in forcefulness of speech.[8] In any case, an attack is made only if the raiders believe that the potential victim has lost his *arutam* soul. If they should fail to kill him, it is because the enemy still retains the soul or had a second one in reserve.

It should be noted that the personal security which the Jívaro believe comes from killing has some social reality. A man who has killed repeatedly, called a *kakaram*, or "powerful one," is rarely attacked, because his enemies feel that the protection provided him by his constantly replaced souls would make any assassination attempt against him fruitless.

Second *arutam* souls can be acquired in several ways. One method is to capture the *arutam* soul of an enemy by beating a log signal drum as previously noted. Another common technique is to walk alone through the forest night after night, without the usual illumination of a copal torch, in the hope of encountering an *arutam* in the darkness. *Arutam* may also be encountered by making a small clearing on a forest mountain top, building a lean-to, and drinking *Datura* there.

Shamans always possess *arutam* souls. Those specializing in betwitching try to steal their intended victim's *arutam* soul before attempting to kill him through witchcraft. If the intended victim is thought to have two *arutam* souls, the shaman asks a shaman "friend" or partner to steal the second one for him, since no one can possess more than two such souls simultaneously. It is believed that shamans, under the influence of *natemä*, can sometimes see a person's *arutam* soul in his chest, where it appears as an inverted rainbow. A shaman, incidentally, does not lose his *arutam* soul when he kills by means of sorcery.

The *arutam* soul must leave a man before he dies, since he cannot die while he retains one (except in the case of contagious disease, in which case retention of the power of two is necessary for certain survival). Thus, at death, he does not have any of the *arutam* souls left which temporarily dwelt in his body while he was alive. Then, at the moment of death, his *own arutam* souls come into existence for the first time. The exact number of these completely new, freshly "born" souls equals the quantity which the deceased person had acquired during his lifetime. Thus, if he had acquired and subsequently lost five *arutam* souls, then at the moment of death he forms five new ones. The formation of these souls is said to generate strong winds, thunder, and lightning in the locality. The newly created *arutam* souls of the dead men will live eternally, drifting as breezes and temporarily entering into the bodies of future generations of Jívaro. At the same moment that these *arutam* souls are "born," the second type of Jívaro soul comes into existence if the deceased person was murdered.

The Muisak[9]

The second kind of soul, the *muisak*, or avenging soul, is closely connected with the *arutam* soul. Only a person who has had an *arutam* soul is capable of forming a *muisak*. Furthermore, a *muisak* comes into existence only when a person who has seen an *arutam* is killed, whether by natural or supernatural means. When such a person is murdered, his avenging soul is created and leaves his corpse through the mouth.[10] If one simply dies of contagious disease or of old age (the latter believed by the Jívaro to be a rare occurrence), no *muisak* is created.

The sole reason for existence of a person's *muisak* is to avenge his death. This soul therefore attempts to kill the murderer, or if this is not possible (due to the murderer having an *arutam* soul), a son or wife of the murderer. The *muisak* is occasionally distracted from this objective, out of jealousy, to kill instead a new spouse of his widow. Because of this latter danger, young men who have not yet acquired much *arutam* power tend to avoid marrying widows.

Technically, the avenging soul is only called a *muisak* while it is in the corpse, subsequently in the shrunken head trophy (*tsantsa*), or its immediate vicinity. When the human head trophy is not taken and prepared, the *muisak* is able to travel as far as it likes from the corpse and to form into one of the three types of *iwanči*, or demons. These three demons are forms of the natural non-human world that can kill a man. One is a particularly dangerous poisonous snake (*makanči*). Another is the water boa constrictor or anaconda (*paɲi*), which can knock over the raft or canoe of the murderer and thereby cause him to drown in the rapid waters of one of the numerous fast-flowing rivers and streams of this hilly country. The third form is a large tree in the forest, which falls on the victim and crushes him. These are the three traditional forms of death in Jívaro society that might be called "accidental" in other cultures. Since the introduction of the machete and of firearms, a belief has been growing that a *muisak* can enter into these items to cause an "accidental" fatal wound. The Jívaro view slight, self-inflicted wounds as true accidents, but grave or fatal self-inflicted wounds are always believed to be the results, respectively, of murder attempts or murders through supernatural mechanisms.

Before the avenging spirit, or *iwanči*, kills the murderer, it sometimes appears to him in the form of a man or a jaguar while he is sleeping. The sleeper tries to seize his firearm or lance (which he keeps on the bed beside him at night) to kill the apparition. Failure to do so will result in the demon eventually succeeding in killing the person. Sometimes this *iwanči* fails in its assassination attempt, only wounding or injuring the intended victim. In such cases, the victim becomes a permanent invalid.

When the demon has performed its act of vengeance, it then appears in a dream to a relative of the victim. In this dream the avenging soul has a human form. Around its neck hangs the shrunken head trophy worn by a killer in the *tsantsa* feast. The demon tells the dreamer, "I have killed an enemy. Now I am going far away, where my relatives are. I am going far away to have a feast with them." The demon disappears and, since it never kills more than a single person, will never murder again.

The widely publicized practice of the Jívaro in shrinking human heads can be well understood only with a knowledge of the *muisak* concept. A major part of the belief and ritual associated with the *tsantsa* is a direct effort to thwart the *muisak* in its mission of vengeance.[11] The Jívaro believe that the completion of the process of headshrinking forces the *muisak*, hovering alongside the retreating war expedition, to enter the head trophy. For this reason, as well as the practical ones that the head would decay if not processed in some way and that the removal of the skull and its contents makes the trophy much lighter to carry on the mountainous trails, the expedition prepares its *tsantsa*(s) as quickly as possible while fleeing the enemy territory. One of the steps in the processing of the shrunken head is to rub charcoal into its skin "so that the *muisak* cannot see out," thereby making it difficult for the avenging soul to plan an "accidental" death in the vicinity of the *tsantsa*.

When the expedition arrives in its home territory, the first feast of the *tsantsa* is held immediately, later followed by at least one and sometimes two others. At all these feasts or dances great care is taken to prevent arguments and fights between the inebriated celebrants out of fear that the *muisak* might take advantage of such an interruption of the magically binding ritual and slip from the head trophy, causing a quarrel to result in a murder. If the feasts are conducted properly, however, the *muisak* will be kept inside of the *tsantsa* until the end of the last feast. At that time, the celebrants expel it from the head trophy and send it back to its neighborhood of origin. This neighborhood is typically at a considerable distance, because head trophies are normally taken only of members of other tribes. As part of this final ritual the women sing:

> Now, now, go back to your house where you lived.
> Your wife is there calling you from your house.
> You have come here to make us happy.
> Finally we have finished.
> So return.

The *tsantsa* is commonly later sold by the head-taker (although illegally in terms of Ecuadorian law) to a mestizo in one of the communities on the western periphery of the tribal territory. At that time, the head-taker silently repeats the exhortation to the *muisak* to return to its distant neighborhood as he hands the *tsantsa* over to the trader. The head-taker goes through this act just in case there is a possibility that the ritual in the *tsantsa* feast did not succeed in its purpose.

During the three feasts the celebrants are concerned with utilizing the power of the *muisak* as well as containing it. As in the case of the *arutam* soul, the *muisak* emits power, but it is believed that the *muisak*'s power is directly transmissible to other persons. The man who took the head holds the *tsantsa* aloft in the ritual dance while two female relatives whom he wants to benefit, most frequently a wife and sister, hold on to him. In this manner the power of the *muisak* is believed to be transmitted to the women, who, ordinarily, lack power-giving *arutam* souls. This power, transmitted from the *muisak* to the women through the "filtering" mechanism of the head-taker, is believed to make it possible for them to work harder and to be more successful in crop production and in the raising of domesticated animals, both of which are primarily the responsibilities of women in Jívaro society.

In addition to the regular head trophy obtained through inter-tribal raiding, there is another kind of *tsantsa* which may, on rare occasions, be made of an *untsuri šuarä* intra-tribal assassination victim, provided he belongs to a neighbor-hood which is consistently hostile to, or very distant from, one's own. To make this *tsantsa*, the killer simply pulls out some of the victim's hair from his head, rather than decapitat-ing him. The hair is loose, not in the form of a scalp, and is then stuck with beeswax onto the top of a tree gourd which has had the bottom cut off. The beeswax, which is nat-urally black, is also used to model eyes, a nose and mouth, and ears on the surface of the calabash. Chonta palm splinters are put through the beeswax lips and a doubled *kumai* bark string is inserted through a hole in the top of the gourd so that the killer may carry it hanging from his neck.

This trophy is used for the regular three feasts, it being believed that the dead enemy's *muisak* is in it because his hair is there. The advantage of this kind of *tsantsa*, according to informants, is that they can make it without getting the blood of members of their own tribe on themselves. It is recognized that making a full-fledged *tsantsa* would be more insulting to the victim's relatives and neighbors and thus more likely to bring large-scale retaliation. Because of the same fear of serious retribution, heads almost never seem to be taken of whites, but several instances are known in which the "hair" *tsantsa* was made from white victims. The Jívaro are frankly uncertain, however, whether whites have *arutam* souls and *muisak*, and it appears that their primary motivation in such cases is to celebrate the killing of whites.

Tsantsa feasts are also held using the shrunken head of a tree sloth. The tree sloth is the only non-human creature thought to be capable of forming a *muisak*. Because the tree sloth moves so slowly, it is said to be very aged and therefore must once have acquired an *arutam* soul to have lived so long. At the same time, since the sloth moves in such a slow manner, it is further believed to have lost its former *arutam* soul(s) and therefore can be killed. The feasting and ritual precautions are basically the same as in the case of a human *tsantsa* but generally somewhat less extensive. The *muisak* of the sloth is believed capable of becoming only a single avenging form, a falling tree.

Sometimes a man who has personally killed someone on an inter-tribal raid has been unable to remove his victim's head before retreating. Under such circumstances, the killer cannot be a full, dancing participant in the first *tsantsa* celebration, but can borrow a *tsantsa* from someone who killed on a previous raid in order to host the two subsequent feasts. Through ritual procedure, the *muisak* of the new victim is believed to be made to enter the old *tsantsa*, and these two *tsantsa* celebrations are called "demon feasts" (*iwanči namper*) in recognition of the presence of the avenging soul of the victim even though a substitute head is being used. Occasionally, a tree sloth *tsantsa* may be used to perform the same function. Normally, however, the tree sloth trophy is made and used by teen-age boys for their first *tsantsa* feasts, which are only two in number and hosted by their fathers or other close older male relatives.

The True Soul

The "true" or "ordinary" soul, the *nekás wakaní*, is born at the same moment as the person and is possessed by every living Jívaro, male or female. The true soul is present in the living individual primarily in the form of one's blood. Bleeding is therefore viewed as a process of soul-loss. This soul is passive during a person's real life and apparently is of relatively little interest to the Jívaro in terms of their total native belief systems.

When a person dies, this true soul leaves his body and, in invisible form, eventually returns to the site of the house where the deceased individual was born. There the soul lives in a spirit house identical to the one in which the deceased was born, except for the fact that the spirit house is invisible to the living. The true souls of other deceased members of the family are likewise dwelling in this house. Similarly, the true souls of former neighbors return to their original house sites as well. It is believed that the true souls conduct their household activities and visit each other just as they did when their possessors were alive. As the years pass, these souls move from house site to house site in the same order, and over the same span of time as they did when incorporated in living individuals.

One significant difference should be noted between this hereafter of the true soul and the real life of its former possessor: these souls are always hungry. Although they engage in subsistence activities and eat what appears to be food to them, it never satisfies them, because it is really just air. The "animals" which these souls hunt in the forest are only the souls of the birds, fish, and mammals which they killed in their former lives. Such an existence of perpetual hunger is the fate of the true souls of all persons, without regard to the kind of life they led while in living individuals. Needless to say, the true soul's fate of persistent starvation is dreaded by the Jívaro.

One can often see deer and owls lingering in the vicinity of abandoned garden and house sites.[12] The Jívaro interpret the presence of such creatures at these old living places as evidence that the animals are temporarily visible embodiments of true souls. The true souls, when they are in these visible forms, are referred to as "human demons" (*šuar iwančï*). There is a moderate fear of them, particularly by women, and the Jívaro taboo on the eating of deer meat is based on the fear that eating such an animal might result in a deceased person's soul entering the body of the living person, with the result that he may subsequently die. These "human demon" animals are often seen in pairs, a fact the Jívaro interpret as indicating that the two creatures are temporarily visible forms of the souls of a man and his wife.

When a true soul has thus repeated the entire life history of its deceased owner, it ceases its existence as a "human demon" and changes into a "true demon." As a true demon, its form is permanently visible and more or less human, although a good deal uglier. The true demon roams the forest hungry, solitary, and lonely, feeling greatly the loss of the company of its former family. When a Jívaro child wanders into the forest and is not found immediately, it is said that a true demon carried off the child because it was so lonely for human companionship. Although it may take the Jívaro two or three days to find the lost child, they almost always succeed, and therefore say that the true demon never harms children, but only wants to play with them.

Then the true demon, after existing for a span of years equivalent to a human lifetime, dies and changes into a certain species of giant butterfly or moth called *wampaŋ*. This creature has markings on its wings which lend it the appearance of an owl's face. All the *wampaŋ* are believed to be souls and are said to be always hungry, as is the case with any of the forms that the true soul takes. When a *wampaŋ* flies inside a house, one of the persons there tosses a small piece of manioc or a few drops of manioc beer in its direction. The Jívaro believe that since the *wampaŋ* might be the soul of a dead relative or friend it would be wrong to neglect its hunger. They do not fear the creature, however.

After a length of time about which the Jívaro are uncertain, the *wampaŋ* finally has its wings damaged by raindrops as it flutters through a rainstorm, and falls to die on the ground. The true soul then changes into water vapor amidst the falling rain. All fog and clouds are believed to be the last form taken by true souls. The true soul undergoes no more transformations and persists eternally in the form of mist.

Of the three kinds of souls in which the Jívaro believe, they seem to be least interested in the "true" one, the *nekás wakanï*, which does little to help the individual survive in his insecure society. It is the *arutam* soul instead that seems to rank first in the Jívaro mind. The *arutam* soul possessor believes himself to be unkillable, thereby gaining a greatly desired sense of security in a social context of continual physical violence and witchcraft, both real and

imagined. Paradoxically, the *arutam* soul concept also en-
dorses assassination as a necessary form of behavior in the
society.

The *arutam* soul belief system contains a number of significant supernatural traits organized together into one internally logical complex. In this system the central idea of
immunity from death is combined with such anthropologi-
cally well-known concepts as: a vision quest; a guardian
spirit; eternal and multiple souls; a variety of generalized
ancestor worship; reincarnation; soul-loss; soul-capture; non-
shamanistic spirit possession; and a concept of personally
acquired impersonal power, *kakarma*, which resembles, but
is not precisely identical to, the Oceanian *mana*.

The concept of the *muisak* furnishes the rationale for
head-taking and shrinking, as well as explaining as supernatural murders those deaths which in many other cultures
would be ascribed to accidental causes. One may observe
that the Jívaro are so preoccupied with killing in physical
life that it seems only consistent that their two most emphasized types of souls, the *muisak* and the *arutam* soul,
are supernatural devices, respectively, for murdering and
avoiding being murdered. Beyond this, it is clear that these
internally coherent and complex bodies of belief are an
important part of the Jívaro view of reality and, as such,
affect their overt behavior.

Shamanism and Illness

The Jívaro believe that witchcraft is the cause of the
vast majority of illnesses and non-violent deaths. Practically
the only diseases not attributed to witchcraft are "white
man's diseases" (*suŋurä*), normally of an epidemic nature,

such as whooping cough, measles, colds, and some mild diarrheas. The normal waking life, as noted before, is simply "a lie," or illusion, while the true forces that determine daily events are supernatural and can only be seen and manipulated with the aid of hallucinogenic drugs. A reality view of this kind creates a demand for shamans, part-time specialists who can cross over into the "real" world at will to help others to deal with the forces that influence and even determine the events of the waking life.

Jívaro shamans (*uwišin*) are of two types: bewitchers and curers. Both kinds take a hallucinogenic drink, whose Jívaro name is *natemä*, in order to enter the supernatural world. This brew, commonly called *yagé* or *yajé* in Colombia, *ayahuasca* (Inca: "vine of the dead") in Ecuador and Peru, and *caapi* in Brazil is prepared from segments of a species of the vine *Banisteriopsis*, a genus belonging to the Malpighiaceae. The Jívaro boil it with the leaves of a similar vine, *yahi*, which probably is also a species of *Banisteriopsis*, to produce the cooled *natemä* tea that contains the powerful hallucinogenic alkaloids harmaline, harmine, d-tetrahydroharmine, and quite possibly N,N-dimethyltryptamine (DMT) (see Plate 22).[18] These compounds have chemical structures and effects similar, but not identical to, LSD, mescaline of the peyote cactus, and psilocybin of the psychotropic Mexican mushroom.

Shamans prefer to use *natemä* rather than *maikua* (*Datura arborea*) for going into trances, because the potency of the latter is too great for the shaman to be able to function ritually in singing, sucking, and the accompanying social interaction. Also, since the shaman must go into trances with frequency, he does not like to use *Datura* for that purpose because the strength of the plant is such that its repeated use is believed to lead to insanity. As an illustration of this danger, one informant said, "My father told me that a long time ago a man took *maikua* all the time. As a result, he lost his mind and would go walking in the forest to speak with the spirits." For these reasons, the shaman tends to use the less strong *Banisteriopsis* drink *natemä*. In *arutam* seeking, however, a person in a trance does not need to perform ritual or interact with others, and therefore *Datura*, precisely because of its strength to produce visions, is the drug of choice.

The use of the hallucinogenic *natemä* drink among the Jívaro makes it possible for almost anyone to achieve the trance state essential for the practice of shamanism. Given the presence of the drug and the felt need to contact the "real," or supernatural, world, it is not surprising that approximately one out of every four Jívaro men is a shaman. Any adult, male or female, who desires to become such a practitioner, simply presents a gift to an already practicing shaman, who administers the *Banisteriopsis* drink and gives some of his own supernatural power—in the form of spirit helpers, or *tsentsak*—to the apprentice. These spirit helpers, or "darts," are the main supernatural forces believed to cause illness and death in daily life. To the non-shaman they are normally invisible, and even shamans can perceive them only under the influence of *natemä*.

The origin of knowledge about the use of *tsentsak* is attributed to Tsuŋi, the mythological first shaman who is believed still to be alive today living underwater in a house whose walls are formed, like palm staves, by upright anacondas, and where he sits, using a turtle as a stool. He is described as a white-skinned man with long hair, but he also seems capable of transforming himself into the anaconda. From time to time he is reputed to supply particular shamans with special quartz crystal *tsentsak* (*namurä*) which are particularly deadly, and, on rare occasions to kill shamans with whom he is angry. No shaman is believed capable of defending himself from the *tsentsak* of Tsuŋi.

Laymen are not able to cure or bewitch, because they do not have these magical darts in their control. Laymen can treat the "white man's diseases," previously mentioned, with herb remedies, but such treatment of illness is little developed in the society. Shamans never use herb remedies.

Shamans send these spirit helpers into the victims' bodies to make them ill or to kill them. At other times, they may suck such spirits sent by enemy shamans from the bodies of tribesmen suffering from witchcraft-induced illness. The spirit helpers also form shields that protect their shaman masters from attacks. The following account presents the ideology of Jívaro shamanism from the point of view of the shamans themselves.

To give the novice some *tsentsak*, the practicing shaman regurgitates what appears to be—to those who have taken *natemä*—a brilliant substance in which the spirit helpers are contained. He cuts part of it off with a machete and gives it to the novice to swallow. The recipient experiences pain upon taking it into his stomach and stays on his bed for ten days, repeatedly drinking *natemä*. The Jívaro believe they can keep magical darts in their stomachs indefinitely and regurgitate them at will. The shaman donating the *tsentsak* periodically blows and rubs all over the body of the novice, apparently to increase the power of the transfer.

The novice must remain inactive and not engage in sexual intercourse for several months. If he fails in self-discipline, as some do, he will not become a successful shaman. At the end of the first month, a *tsentsak* emerges from his mouth. With this magical dart at his disposal, the new shaman experiences a tremendous desire to bewitch. If he casts his *tsentsak* to fulfill this desire, this means he will become a "bewitching" shaman (*wawek*, or *yahaučï uwišin*). If, on the other hand, the novice can control his impulse and reswallow this first *tsentsak*, he will become a curing shaman (*peŋer uwišin*). This will only be possible if the shaman who gave him his *tsentsak* is a curer himself.

If the shaman who gave the *tsentsak* to the new man was primarily a bewitcher, rather than a curer, the novice likewise will become a bewitcher. This is because a bewitcher's magical darts have such a desire to kill that their new owner will be compelled to adopt their attitude. One informant said that the urge to kill felt by bewitching shamans came to them with a strength and frequency similar to that of hunger.

Only if the novice shaman is able to abstain from sexual intercourse for five months, will he have the power to kill a man (if he is a bewitcher) or cure a victim (if he is a curer). A full year's abstinence is considered necessary to become a really effective bewitcher or curer.

During the period of sexual abstinence, the new shaman collects all kinds of insects, plants, and other objects, which he now has the power to convert into *tsentsak*. Almost any object, including living insects and worms, can become a *tsentsak* if it is small enough to be swallowed by a shaman. Certain small spiders become *tunčï*, a special kind of *tsentsak*. Different types of *tsentsak* are used to cause different kinds and degrees of illness, and the greater the variety of these objects that a shaman has in his body, the greater is his ability.

According to Jívaro concepts, each *tsentsak* has a natural and a supernatural aspect. The magical dart's natural aspect is that of an ordinary material object as seen without drinking the drug *natemä*. But the supernatural and "true" aspect of the *tsentsak* is revealed to the shaman by taking *natemä*. When he does this, the magical darts appear in new forms as demons and with new names. In their supernatural aspects, the *tsentsak* are not simply objects but spirit helpers in various forms, such as giant butterflies, jaguars, or monkeys, who actively assist the shaman in his tasks.

Bewitching is carried out against a specific, known individual and thus is usually done to neighbors or, at the most, fellow tribesmen. Normally, as is the case with intra-tribal assassination, bewitching is done to avenge a particular offense committed against one's family or friends. Both bewitching and individual assassination contrast with the large-scale head-hunting raids conducted against entire households of enemy tribes.

To bewitch, the shaman takes *natemä* and secretly approaches the house of his victim. Just out of sight in the forest, he drinks green tobacco water, enabling him to regurgitate a *tsentsak*, which he throws as his victim comes out of his house. If the *tsentsak* is strong enough and is thrown with sufficient force, it will pass all the way through the victim's body, causing death within a period of a few days to several weeks. More often, however, the magical dart simply lodges in the victim's body. If the shaman, in his hiding place, fails to see the intended victim, he may instead bewitch any member of the intended victim's family who appears, usually a wife or child. When the shaman's mission is accomplished, he returns secretly to his own home.

One of the distinguishing characteristics of the bewitching process among the Jívaro is that, as far as could be learned, the victim is given no specific indication that someone is bewitching him. The bewitcher does not want his victim to be aware that he is being supernaturally attacked, lest he take protective measures by immediately procuring the services of a curing shaman. Nonetheless, shamans and laymen alike steadfastly claimed, in interviews, that illness invariably follows the bewitchment, although the degree of illness can vary considerably.

A special kind of spirit helper, called a *pasuk*, can aid the bewitching shaman by remaining near the victim in the guise of an insect or animal of the forest after the bewitcher has left. This spirit helper has his own objects to shoot into the victim should a curing shaman succeed in sucking out the *tsentsak* sent earlier by the bewitcher who is the owner of the *pasuk*.

In addition, the bewitcher can enlist the aid of a *wakani* ("soul," or "spirit") bird. Shamans have the power to call these birds and use them as spirit helpers in bewitching victims. The shaman blows on the *wakani* birds and then sends them to the house of the victim to fly around and around the man, frightening him. This is believed to cause fever and insanity, with death resulting shortly thereafter.

After he returns home from bewitching, the shaman may send a *wakani* bird to perch near the house of the victim. Then, if a curing shaman sucks out the intruding object, the bewitching shaman sends the *wakani* bird more *tsentsak* to throw from its beak into the victim. By continually re-supplying the *wakani* bird with new *tsentsak*, the sorcerer makes it impossible for the curer to rid his patient per-manently of the magical darts.

While the *wakani* birds are supernatural servants avail-able to anyone who wishes to use them, the *pasuk*, chief among the spirit helpers, serves only a single shaman. Like-wise a shaman possesses only one *pasuk*. The *pasuk*, being specialized for the service of bewitching, has a protective shield to guard it from counterattack by the curing shaman.

The curing shaman, under the influence of *natemä*, sees the *pasuk* of the bewitcher in human form and size, but "covered with iron except for its eyes." The curing shaman can kill this *pasuk* only by shooting a *tsentsak* into its eyes, the sole vunerable area in the *pasuk*'s armor. To the person who has not taken the hallucinogenic drink, the *pasuk* usually appears to be simply a tarantula.

Shamans may also kill or injure a person by using magical darts, *anamuk*, to create supernatural animals that attack a victim. If a shaman has a small, pointed armadillo bone *tsentsak*, he can shoot this into a river while the victim is crossing it on a balsa raft or in a canoe. Under the water, this bone manifests itself in its supernatural aspect as an anaconda, which rises up and overturns the craft, causing the victim to drown. The shaman can similarly use a tooth from a killed snake as a *tsentsak*, creating a poisonous serpent to bite his victim. In more or less the same manner, shamans can create jaguars and pumas to kill their victims.

About five years after receiving his *tsentsak*, a bewitching shaman undergoes a test to see if he still retains enough *tsentsak* power to continue to kill successfully. This test involves bewitching a tree. The shaman, under the influence of *natemä*, attempts to throw a *tsentsak* through the tree at the point where its two main branches join. If his strength and aim are adequate, the tree appears to split the moment the *tsentsak* is sent into it. The splitting, however, is invisible to an observer who is not under the influence of the hallucinogen. If the shaman fails, he knows that he is incapable of killing a human victim. This means that, as soon as possible, he must go to a strong shaman and purchase a new supply of *tsentsak*. Until he has the goods with which to pay for this new supply, he is in constant danger, in his proved weakened condition, of being seriously bewitched by other shamans. Therefore, each day, he drinks large quantities of *natemä*, tobacco water, and the extract of yet another drug, *pirípiri*. He also rests on his bed at home to conserve his strength, but tries to conceal his weakened condition from his enemies. When he purchases a new supply of *tsentsak*, he can safely cut down his consumption of these other substances.

The degree of illness produced in a witchcraft victim is a function of both the force with which the *tsentsak* is shot into the body, and also of the character of the magical dart itself. If a *tsentsak* is shot all the way through the body of a victim, then "there is nothing for a curing shaman to suck out," and the patient dies. If the magical dart lodges within the body, however, it is theoretically possible to cure the victim by sucking. But in actual practice, the sucking is not always considered successful.

The work of the curing shaman is complementary to that of a bewitcher. When a curing shaman is called in to treat a patient, his first task is to see if the illness is due to witchcraft. The usual diagnosis and treatment begin with the curing shaman drinking *natemä*, tobacco water, and *pirípiri* in the late afternoon and early evening. These drugs permit him to see into the body of the patient as though it were glass. If the illness is due to sorcery, the curing shaman will see the intruding object within the patient's body clearly enough to determine whether or not he can cure the sickness (see Plate 23).

A shaman sucks magical darts from a patient's body only at night, and in a dark area of the house, for it is only in the dark that he can perceive the drug-induced visions that are the supernatural reality. With the setting of the sun,

he alerts his *tsentsak* by whistling the tune of the curing
song; after about a quarter of an hour, he starts singing.
A shaman's curing songs tend to be self-encouraging ex-
hortations such as the following:

> I, I, I, I, I,
> I, I, I, I.
> I am like Tsuŋi.[14]
> I am like Tsuŋi.
> When I drink *natemä*
> All my body becomes cold.
> And I easily suck out the *tsentsak*.
> I, I, I, I.
>
> I am always above the clouds,
> And thus I have power.
> I drank *natemä*.
> I drank enough to have power.
> All my body is cold.
> Therefore I have power to suck out the *tsentsak*.
> I, I, I, I.
>
> There is a very large body of water.
> Thus I am like a great body of water.
> I have a crown, but of gold,
> Brilliant.[15]
> How beautiful it appears
> When I drink *natemä*.
> Therefore it is easy to suck out the *tsentsak*.
> I, I, I, I.
>
> I am always above the clouds.
> Therefore I cure easily.
> I have the *tsentsak* of *natemä*.
> I am seated, but I am very cold
> And there are many breezes.[16]
> I, I, I, I.

My *tsentsak* are like birds
And the wings and bodies are dreams.
With these I am now ready.
My *tsentsak* are sitting all over me[17]
And as I become cold
I shall have power.
I can easily suck out *tsentsak*.
I, I, I, I.

I am like some *payü* of the Río Napo.[18]
Therefore I have power to suck out *tsentsak*.
I, I, I, I.

Wait, wait a moment.
Now I am going to become dizzy.
I will see when I am intoxicated.

When he is ready to suck, the shaman regurgitates two *tsentsak* into the sides of his throat and mouth. These must be identical to the one he has seen in the patient's body. He holds one of these in the front of the mouth and the other in the rear. They are expected to catch the supernatural aspect of the magical dart that the shaman sucks out of the patient's body. The *tsentsak* nearest the shaman's lips is supposed to incorporate the sucked-out *tsentsak* essence within itself. If, however, this supernatural essence should get past it, the second magical dart in the mouth blocks the throat so that the intruder cannot enter the interior of the shaman's body. If the curer's two *tsentsak* were to fail to catch the supernatural essence of the *tsentsak*, it would pass down into the shaman's stomach and kill him. Trapped thus within the mouth, this essence is shortly caught by, and incorporated into, the material substance of one of the curing shaman's *tsentsak*. He then "vomits" out this object and displays it to the patient and his family, saying, "Now I have sucked it out. Here it is."

The non-shamans think that the material object itself is what has been sucked out, and the shaman does not disillusion them. At the same time, he is not lying, because he knows that the only important thing about a *tsentsak* is its supernatural aspect, or essence, which he sincerely believes he has removed from the patient's body. To explain to the layman that he already had these objects in his mouth would serve no fruitful purpose and would prevent him from displaying such an object as proof that he had cured the patient. Without incontrovertible evidence, he would not be able to convince the patient and his family that he had effected the cure and must be paid.

The ability of the shaman to suck depends largely upon the quantity and strength of his own *tsentsak*, of which he may have hundreds. His magical darts assume their supernatural aspect as spirit helpers when he is under the influence of *natemä*, and he sees them as a variety of zoomorphic forms hovering over him, perching on his shoulders, sticking out of his skin, and helping to suck the patient's body. He must drink tobacco water every few hours to "keep them fed" so that they will not leave him. He will also appear, to another shaman under the influence of *natemä*, to have a gold, red and greenish "crown" above his head (see Plate 24).

The curing shaman must also deal with any *pasuk* that may be in the patient's vicinity for the purpose of casting more darts. He drinks additional amounts of *natemä* in order to see them and engages in *tsentsak* duels with them if they are present. While the *pasuk* is enclosed in iron armor, the shaman himself has his own armor, composed of his many *tsentsak*. As long as he is under the influence of *natemä*, these magical darts cover his body as a protective shield, and are on the lookout for any enemy *tsentsak* headed towards their master. When these *tsentsak* see such a missile coming, they immediately close up together at the point where the enemy dart is attempting to penetrate, and thereby repel it.

If the curer finds *tsentsak* entering the body of his patient after he has killed the *pasuk*, he suspects the presence of a *wakanï* bird. The shaman drinks *maikua* (*Datura*), since it is more powerful than *natemä*, as well as tobacco water, and silently sneaks into the forest to hunt and kill the bird with *tsentsak*. When he succeeds, the curer returns to the patient's home, blows all over the house to get rid of the "atmosphere" created by the numerous *tsentsak* sent by the bird, and completes his sucking of the patient. Even after all the *tsentsak* are extracted, the shaman may remain another night at the house to suck out any "dirtiness" (*pahuri*) still inside. In the cures which I have witnessed, this sucking is a most noisy process, accompanied by deep, but dry, vomiting.

After sucking out a *tsentsak*, the shaman puts it into a little container. He does not swallow it, because it is not his own magical dart and would therefore kill him. Later, he throws the *tsentsak* into the air, and it flies back to the shaman who sent it originally into the patient. *Tsentsak* also fly back to a shaman at the death of a former apprentice who had originally received them from him. Besides receiving "old" magical darts unexpectedly in this manner, the shaman may have *tsentsak* thrown at him by a bewitcher. Accordingly, shamans constantly drink tobacco water at all hours of the day and night. Although the tobacco water is not truly hallucinogenic, it produces a narcotized state, which is believed necessary to keep one's *tsentsak* ready to repel any other magical darts. A shaman does not even dare go for a walk without taking along the green tobacco leaves with which he prepares the juice that keeps his spirit helpers alert. Less frequently, but regularly, he must drink *natemä* for the same purpose and to keep in touch with the supernatural reality.

While curing under the influence of *natemä*, the curing shaman "sees" the shaman who bewitched his patient. Generally, he can recognize the person, unless it is a shaman who lives far away or in another tribe. The patient's family knows this, and demands to be told the identity of the bewitcher, particularly if the sick person dies. At one curing session I attended, the shaman could not identify the person he had seen in his vision. The brother of the dead man then accused the shaman himself of being responsible. Under such pressure, there is a strong tendency for the curing shaman to attribute each case to a particular bewitcher.

Shamans gradually become weak and must purchase *tsentsak* again and again. Curers tend to become weak in power especially after curing a patient bewitched by a shaman who has recently received a new supply of magical darts. Thus the most powerful shamans are those who can repeatedly purchase new supplies of *tsentsak* from other shamans, particularly *payü* (see pp. 119–20).

Shamans can take back *tsentsak* from others to whom they have previously given them. To accomplish this, the shaman drinks *natemä*, and, using his *tsentsak*, creates a "bridge" in the form of a rainbow between himself and the other shaman. Then he shoots a *tsentsak* along this rainbow. This strikes the ground beside the other shaman with an explosion and flash likened to a lightning bolt. The purpose of this is to surprise the other shaman so that he temporarily forgets to maintain his guard over his magical darts, thus permitting the first shaman to suck them back along the rainbow. A shaman who has had his *tsentsak* taken away in this manner will discover that "nothing happens" when he drinks *natemä*. The sudden loss of his *tsentsak* will tend to make him ill, but ordinarily the illness is not fatal unless a be-witcher shoots a magical dart into him while he is in this weakened condition. If he has not become disillusioned by his experience, he can again purchase *tsentsak* from some other shaman and resume his calling.

Death

A death is announced to the neighborhood by beating the log signal drum, if the house has one, in the same rhythm used to send the alarm when a house is attacked. Little ambiguity usually is involved since the neighbors tend to know whether anyone in the signaling household has been seriously ill. All corpses are buried inside of the house instead of out of doors so as to "keep the dead one protected from the cold rain." Except when the house owner dies, the family continues to live in the dwelling, the rationale being expressed thus by an informant: "When they were alive, we did not fear them. Therefore we should not fear them when they are dead, although we do a little." After the house is later abandoned in the normal course of events, family members will return when the roof seriously disintegrates to build a small palm thatch over the grave.

If an infant or small child dies, the body is put into a large beer-brewing jar or cooking pot in an upright sitting position. An inverted cooking pot is placed on top to act as a cover, and the two vessels are sealed together with clay. The urn is bur-ied in the center of the house with some chonta palm staves laid above it to protect the pottery cover from being crushed by persons walking above.

The bodies of deceased older children and wives are also buried in the house floor, although not in urns. A body is interred on its back and extended, with the arms at the sides, and wrapped in sections of split guadua bamboo. More split bamboo is laid on top before the earth is added. Graves are usually only about two-and-a-half to three feet deep, one man explaining, "When we live, we do not live far away from the surface of the earth, so when we are dead, we should not, either."

When the house owner dies, the dwelling is abandoned and his wife (wives) and children will go or be taken to live with other relatives, such as a potential husband (*yači* of the deceased) or a son-in-law, until she remarries. She cuts her hair short as a sign of mourning, and ideally should not take a new husband until the hair has grown back down to her shoulders. Since the house will no longer be used, the deceased head of the household may be buried either below ground or above it on a low scaffold. In the latter case, a large balsa log is hollowed out in a manner somewhat similar to a canoe, from which it takes its name (*kanu*), although canoes are not actually used for this purpose. The corpse is laid inside and the coffin top is covered with lashed-down bark from the same log. Finally, the log is placed on crossbars so that it is between, and in line with, the two main center posts of the house, with the head towards the doorway of the women's end of the dwelling. A grave is in the same location. If several persons in a household die simultaneously in an epidemic and, as a result, the house is abandoned, they may all receive a scaffold burial.

Whether buried above or below ground, a man's corpse is dressed in a new kilt, adorned with his glass bead necklaces, and two black streaks are painted under his eyes. The body is wrapped in a woman's dress, the largest cloth available. A palm-wood fighting lance is laid parallel to his body on the surface of the ground, and on the ground adjacent to the burial is placed the man's round stool. From a house beam overhead is suspended his monkey skin traveling bag containing his combs, ornamental earsticks, and knife or machete blade fragment.

If the deceased male still had a *tsantsa* in his possession, it is interred with him, under his back. Conversely, if he himself was the victim of a head-taking raid, his corpse is buried in the usual way.

A woman is buried in her finest dress and wearing her snail shell dance belt, glass bead necklaces, toucan feather earrings, and an ornamental stick in her lower lip. Her pottery-making tools and beer strainer are placed on the ground near her head, and one of her carrying baskets, containing personal effects, such as her comb and perfume bundle, is hung from a house beam above.

A large basket of cooked manioc and meat is left hanging above the head of the deceased, whether male or female, and a bowl of manioc beer is placed on the ground. The food and beer are replaced daily for about a week, after which it is believed that the *nekás wakaní*, the true soul, has normally departed. However, if one of the survivors subsequently has a bad dream in which the deceased appears and complains of not being fed, the food and beer containers are hastily replenished.

Occasionally, an elderly, outstanding *untä* with renown as a killer may, on his deathbed, advise one or more sons that he wants them each to acquire one of his own *arutam* souls, which form at his death. When he dies, his corpse is entombed in a special way. It is seated on his round stool, leaning against the center post in the men's end of the abandoned house, facing the doorway. A chonta palm stave stockade is erected all around the body, about one foot from it. A small opening is made in the front of the stockade through which is inserted the magical balsa wood staff the deceased used in bathing at the sacred waterfall. The staff touches a bare spot, left uncovered, on the chest of the corpse and extends horizontally out through the barrier.

In the adjacent forest, the sons build small lean-to's, each about 300 yards away in the four cardinal directions. Each night a son can come to the abandoned house to seek an *arutam* soul created by the dead father which, hopefully, is wandering in the vicinity. The seeker must come alone, without a copal torch, and in the utter darkness of the house touch the magical staff, follow it with his hand until he contacts the dead man's chest, and say, "I am your son, Father." He then goes out of the house to the north lean-to where he drinks tobacco water (nothing stronger is used) and awaits an *arutam* for about two hours. If none appears, he returns to the house, repeats the ritual and goes to the south lean-to, where he takes more tobacco water. The same procedure is repeated for the east and west lean-to's, dawn finding the *arutam* seeker at the last place unless he has already been successful.

On the subsequent night, another son, or even a son-in-law of the deceased, may visit the corpse, explain his kin relationship and attempt to see an *arutam*. According to several accounts, the vision is often seen not only in the lean-to's, but in the house, where the *arutam* souls are believed to come back to visit. Usually the corpse is left in this upright position only two days and then buried in the usual manner, although there are cases where it has been left longer.

Chapter V

LAW, FEUDING, AND WAR

I was born to die fighting.

Jívaro saying

On an abstract level, there is near unanimity among the interior Jívaro as to what is correct, normative social behavior. In any specific case, however, there is usually radical disagreement as to whether a particular anti-social act was justified as a punitive sanction in reprisal for some past offense, or whether it was, in fact, an unjustified act which itself deserves the application of retaliatory punitive sanctions. This situation, of course, is quite understandable in a society where there is no state, no chiefdom, no corporate kin groups, and, really, no locus of authority which can impose judicial decisions and enforce them.

An additional factor of no minor significance is that a high proportion of persons who have been accused of hostile acts probably did not commit them at all, but there is no way of satisfactorily demonstrating their "guilt" or "innocence." This situation is primarily due to the tremendous emphasis among the Jívaro on ascribing almost all non-epidemic illnesses and deaths, and non-violent deaths, to witchcraft and poisoning. The fundamental assumption, not surprising in the absence of modern medical knowledge and in the presence of the tensions previously discussed, is that bewitching shamans are continually attacking one's person and family. This leads, in the cases of assumed witchcraft death, to punitive retaliatory sanctions, in the form of homicide, against the presumed bewitchers. With the guilt determined through divination with the aid of a hallucinogenic drug, and the subsequent vengeance probably wreaked on the wrong person (even if one believes in witchcraft deaths), it is clear that the shamanistic beliefs and practices have repercussions which heighten the sense of outrage and injustice that permeates the society and sets household against household. Under these circumstances, Jívaro witchcraft clearly promotes rather than decreases physical violence.

Although not believed by the Jívaro to be quite as pervasive an activity as bewitching, assumed poisoning in beer or in food likewise engenders retaliatory action through physical violence, even though, as in the case of witchcraft, the person believed to be guilty is, more likely than not, probably innocent. Under these conditions, then, the relatively clear-cut and consensually approved rules concerning offenses and sanctions regarding human life, sexual relationships, inheritance of women, and other less emphasized areas of dispute, have only limited utility in promoting social harmony and tranquillity.

Since there is no formal political or kin organization, the Jívaro apply sanctions against alleged violators of the norms purely by means of informal partisan action. The aggrieved party, together with those relatives willing to support him, takes upon himself the responsibility for punishing the person or persons he believes to be guilty of an offense against him or a close member of his family.

The determination of guilt in a specific case and of the proper sanction for a specific offense is a rather individualistic matter, with a significant degree of variability existing in case histories of even a single type of offense. The emphasis in the present description will be on the general pattern of offenses and sanctions, rather than on deviations from the norms.

Rights, Offenses, and Sanctions

It is considered wrong to kill or injure other persons within the tribe unless it is to punish someone for a similar act, in which case precise equivalence in retribution is justified. Most deaths are considered to be cases of homicide, whether through actual physical violence (including poisoning), bewitching, or by avenging souls (*muisak*) of the dead. While no retaliation is attempted in the case of deaths believed to be caused by *muisak*, retaliation by assassination is definitely considered to be in order when a member of one's conjugal family is murdered through physical violence or witchcraft.

According to Jívaro norms, approved sanctions are an approximation of equivalent retaliation against the guilty party himself or a member of his immediate family, such as a brother, wife, or child. Thus the sanction against homicide is homicide. Although such sanctions are directed primarily at adult males, partially because it is not considered particularly honorable or desirable to kill women or children within the tribe, the punitive assassins may kill their intended victim's wife or child if they fail to find him at home when they make their vengeance raid. It is also considered completely proper to kill a woman or child if the act is in retaliation for the previous murder of a woman or child. Great pains are usually taken to kill only one person in retaliation for one murder. This situation of intra-tribal retaliation on a one-to-one basis should be clearly distinguished from the head-taking raids against the Achuara tribe, which involve killing as many of the "aliens" as possible.

If there is a considerable lapse of time before administering a sanction, the guilty party may, after a few years, send a shotgun to the aggrieved party as a compensation to terminate the matter. If the aggrieved party, primarily considered to be the eldest male of the murdered man's conjugal family, accepts this gift, then the gift-receiver takes the responsibility for seeing that his kinsmen consider that the matter is finished. He warns the other relatives of the dead man that if they attempt to kill the gift-giver for the old offense, they will have to fight him (the gift-receiver) as well.

While sanctions against murder by physical violence are, in return, expected to be by physical violence, punitive assassination of one who has murdered through bewitching may be either by means of sorcery or physical violence. Normally, the sanction for a first murder offense by means of sorcery is also assassination by sorcery. For a second homicidal sorcery offense, physical violence is considered to be the more proper sanction.

The importance of the concept of equivalent retaliation is indicated by the sanction considered proper when a man is poisoned by a woman. Poisoning (one of the favorite forms of murder) is done almost exclusively by women, since they alone prepare and serve the food and beer to guests. When a man is fatally poisoned, the aggrieved family may not attempt to kill the guilty woman, if they feel that the death of a woman would be inadequate to compensate for the death of a man. In such a case, they assume that the proper sanction is to poison the guilty woman's brother. Often, however, the vengeance is wreaked directly on the woman believed responsible. They usually have to wait several years in order to catch the victim off guard at a feast in order to poison him or her successfully.

In both poisoning and sorcery, there is the problem of properly identifying the guilty party. Most poisoning is done at the large *tsantsa* victory feasts, where a dozen or more women of different households are continually circulating among the guests serving manioc beer. The poisoner, under such circumstances, is very difficult to detect. The family of the victim, however, invariably accepts the opinion of the dying victim as to the identity of the guilty party, and her brother is marked for death.

A curing shaman who has attempted unsuccessfully to cure a fatal case of sorcery is expected to tell the deceased's survivors the identity of the bewitching shaman. Sometimes the shaman does so, but at least as often he simply says that the fatal magical dart came from a shaman "far away" whom he cannot recognize. In this way, informants say, the shaman avoids the reprisals which might result against himself if he were to name a specific Jívaro as the guilty party.

It is not believed proper to assassinate personally a brother or trading partner in retaliation even for the murder of one's wife or child, although cases do occur. The more common approach to administering the punishment is for the aggrieved party to plan and organize the avenging raid without actually participating. In such a situation, a non-related or distantly related *kakaram* may be invited to come and carry out the assassination.

Murder by witchcraft requires the sanction of homicide by physical violence, but most non-fatal illnesses ascribed to witchcraft do not usually evoke retaliation. One reason is that normally a curing shaman does not reveal the identity of the bewitcher except in fatal cases. When retaliation is desired for non-fatal witchcraft illnesses, the recovered patient hires a bewitching shaman to bewitch the original bewitcher.

Sexual offenses, with the exception of wife-stealing, normally do not involve the sanction of homicide. The punishment varies in specific instances, but most commonly consists of slashing the forehead and scalp of the offender with a machete. Ordinarily, the aggrieved party administers the punishment personally while several relatives hold the victim. The slashing is usually done without much care, and sometimes the offender dies, although this result is not intended. In the case of premarital sexual intercourse, the punishment is administered to the girl and her lover by the girl's father. In the case of adultery, a man primarily punishes his wife's lover, and a woman primarily punishes her husband.

Premarital intercourse is a less serious offense than extramarital. Premarital sexual relations are widespread, and single girls frequently become pregnant. Such affairs usually are looked upon fairly tolerantly by everyone, even by a girl's mother, as long as the girl's father does not discover them in the act. If such a discovery occurs, the father has to punish them in order to avoid becoming the butt of jokes in the neighborhood. The father is expected to slash the scalps of both under such circumstances.

When a man learns that another has had sexual relations with his wife, he has the right to cut her lover's scalp whether he discovered him in the act or not. Unlike the punishment for murder, this cutting is usually administered immediately by the aggrieved party, accompanied by several of his kinsmen, normally brothers, parallel or cross-cousins, or his father. If the adulterer flees to a distant neighborhood or otherwise prevents them from punishing him, then the aggrieved party may, in his anger, kill the father of the adulterer, or, if he is not living, a brother or cousin (parallel or cross).

Even if the punishers are successful in their slashing of the offender's forehead or scalp, they and their close relatives usually remain angry with the family of the offender and refuse to speak to them. After about two years, the offender is also expected to pay the husband a toucan feather headband of the *tawaspä* type (worth approximately one shotgun) and strings of beads. This formally terminates the matter.

Seduction of one's wife by one's brother usually does not seem to be considered quite as grave an offense as ordinary adultery. It still warrants a slashing of the offender's head, but the cutting sometimes is done with just a toucan beak instead of a machete. An offender who is a brother of the husband never has to pay anything in addition.

In cases where the husband discovers the offense at the moment of commission, his anger affects the degree of variability from the norm in the actual manner of punishment. Thus sometimes the husband may kill the offender or mutilate the genitalia of the woman. Ordinarily, however, the wife is not punished, particularly when she is not caught in the act and when she is the one who informs the husband of the incident.

Rape is not recognized as such and informants could recall no case of a woman violently resisting sexual intercourse. They said that a man would never commit such an act if the woman resisted, because she would tell her family and they would then punish him. Also, it seems that both men and women tend to regard adultery as a spicy diversion, whose attraction seems to be sufficient to make rape unnecessary.

A woman has the right to punish a husband guilty of adultery. If she actually discovers him in the act, she is expected to slash his scalp with a machete. She rarely attacks the other woman. The husband thus slashed goes to live at the house of his father, or of an avuncular relative called father, or of a brother. Usually after about a month, his wife sends him the message that if he wants to return to her, he should do so immediately or she will cut his head again. If she does not thus invite him to return, however, he remains separated.

If a man repeatedly commits adultery, his wife has the right to poison him. Of course, the brothers and other close relatives of the man will attempt to murder her in retaliation. Poisoning is also the sanction against a woman who deserts her husband. Desertion of a wife by a man is virtually unheard of, except when she is implacably hostile towards him, in which case it is proper for him to leave.

Incest is a sexual offense that merits different degrees of punishment depending upon the degree of relationship. Sexual intercourse with any known relative other than a cross-cousin (*wahe*), or a more distant relative also classified as a *wahe*, is considered to be some degree of incest. If such a pair marries, they lose the respect of the neighborhood, and are called jokingly, *aka* (a species of worm) because, as one informant said, "worms enter wherever they like." The couple will be told, "We don't want *aka* to multiply here. Go to live far away." Although the couple is embarrassed, they ordinarily remain in the same neighborhood.

Deemed far more serious are cases of incest within the conjugal family, i.e., between parents and their children or between siblings. If a man is found to have had intercourse with his daughter, one of the girl's *wahe* (male cross-cousin and potential mate) has the right to beat him with his fists. Then the father usually leaves the neighborhood and also his wife separates from him. If a man has intercourse with his own sister, a brother has the right to slash his head, and to tell him to leave the neighborhood. If there is no brother, it is the duty of the father. If the father is not living, a male cross-cousin has the right to beat, but not to slash, the offender.

Clearly defined norms exist regarding the inheritance of

both wives and material goods, although disputes regarding the latter category tend to be minor. The deceased man's eldest brother has the right to inherit his wife (wives). If there is no surviving brother of the deceased man, then his eldest parallel cousin is entitled to inherit the wife (wives). If the deceased man lacks sons of post-puberty age, his eldest brother also inherits his possessions. Otherwise, the eldest son receives these goods. There is a mild feeling that the eldest brother inheriting plural wives, or the eldest son inheriting material possessions, should distribute some of his new wealth to each of his younger brothers as they pass puberty.

Violation of the levirate, the right of a man to marry his deceased younger brother's widow, is a serious and common offense since there is great competition for recent widows. If a man marries a widow without first paying a shotgun to her deceased husband's eldest brother, or to the eldest male parallel cousin if there are no brothers, then the eldest brother or parallel cousin has the right to kill him.

On the other hand, if a brother or parallel cousin of the deceased man takes her away after she has moved into the household of a new husband, the latter has the right to kill the abductor as a wife-stealer. Wife-stealing is a capital offense and leads, as does presumed bewitching, to many of the killings and feuds.

A woman's property is inherited by her eldest daughter. If there is no daughter, the deceased girl's mother inherits the possessions. When there is neither a surviving daughter nor mother, a sister of the deceased girl may have the possessions if she asks for them. Otherwise, the widower keeps the things to give to a future wife.

Offenses involving material property are not common. Stealing, for example, is virtually unheard of with the exception of household looting following the assassination of an enemy. In such cases, the assassins are practicing behavior which is supposed to be reserved for acts of war against non-*untsuri šuarä*. Such behavior is thus in the nature of an additional indignity inflicted upon the victim's household, and is normally considered very bad form within the tribe. Inheritance of property does not always go entirely smoothly, however, because younger siblings may be angered if the eldest does not share some of the inheritance. Since, however, the eldest has the legal right to keep all the parent's possessions, the younger siblings do not have any recourse to any formalized sanctions. They usually just refuse to visit the elder brother.

A man's property consists of the house he has built, the artifacts that he has made or has received as gifts, the game and fish that he has caught, and the crops (mainly maize) that he has raised. A woman's property likewise consists of the artifacts she has made or received as gifts, wild foods she has gathered, the crops that she is cultivating or has harvested, the section of the garden in which she raises them (if there is another wife), and the pigs and chickens that she raises. A woman may also own a pottery clay deposit if it is near her house and she was its discoverer and excavator.

Land, or natural resources, is not owned individually or communally, except in the sense that a specific garden or part of a garden is owned by a woman as long as it is being cultivated, usually no more than about five years. Even in this case, it is the capital improvement of the land that is owned, in the form of the garden, not the land in its natural state. No territorial boundaries are recognized for hunting, fishing,[1] or other purposes on a tribal, neighborhood, or household level except in one type of apparently very rare situation. This was a reported case of two related men living a few hundred feet apart who agreed to consider a small stream which ran between their houses as a boundary for purposes of clearing land for their wives' gardens.

Feuding

Due to the retaliatory nature of Jívaro legal sanctions, the application of any avenging action is likely to initiate long and drawn-out hostilities between two groups of kinsmen. This pattern of repeated application of sanctions by two families against one another is a dominant preoccupation in interior Jívaro life.

Such feuding is a state of mind as much as a pattern of overt behavior. Both of the parties concerned feel that the other family has not been properly punished for past wrong-doings. These feelings are evident from the daily conversations in which individuals continually remind their families of the wrongs committed against them or their close relatives. At the same time they stress their own personal interest in maintaining peace. This avowed personal desire for peace is apparently intended in part to impress the listener with the non-malicious character of the speaker. Despite common avowals of peaceful intentions, however, hostile acts are committed sufficiently often that throughout the interior region house doors are generally barred at night, men sleep with their guns at their sides, rarely go more than a few hundred feet from their houses without weapons, and when visiting another family, expect their hostess to sample the beer, before she serves it, to prove it is not poisoned. In households that are momentarily expecting an assassination raid against them, no one ventures outside the house after dark under any circumstances, and bodily needs are attended to on the floor of the house, the soiled spot to be dug up and removed the next day.

The initiation of a feud does not formally occur until one of the parties sends the message to the other, "Let us fight with guns. . . ." Such a message is sent normally after the two parties have (or are alleged to have) each poisoned or bewitched one of the opposite group or to have stolen a wife from it. The first party to have allegedly poisoned, bewitched, or to have stolen a wife, then sends the formal invitation to have recourse to guns. Such an invitation is unnecessary in cases where homicides have already been effected by force of arms. This invitation is not a warning of an attack, since generally three to five years then pass before the assassination attempt actually occurs. Rather, it is a public statement of the legal justification for an attack at some future time. The actual assassination raid itself, when it does occur, is conducted in the utmost secrecy.

In view of the emotional intensity of the feuding, it is not surprising that when a man "no longer wants to live," he does not commit suicide in the ordinary sense, but rather suddenly starts leading assassination raids against the men who are his enemies, insisting on taking the principal risks, such as being the first to charge into the enemy's house. Sooner or later, of course, he will himself be killed, which apparently surprises no one, since his self-destructive bent is seen as evidence that he no longer possesses an *arutam* soul. That this kind of "suicide" appeals to Jívaro men is indicated by the fact that while cases of it are fairly well known, not a single one could be found of self-inflicted suicide by a male. In contrast, self-inflicted suicide by women, mainly by hanging from a house beam, is relatively common. Acts of suicide by women occurred, according to informants of both sexes, when they were consistently treated badly and beaten by their husbands, or when they had been discovered committing adultery and were fearful of being slashed on the head or otherwise mutilated by their irate spouses.

Feuds can be formally ended by payment, provided that the last killing occurred sufficiently long ago for the deceased's relatives to be willing to settle for less than a retaliatory killing. In all cases, only one person is paid, usually the oldest male relative in the closest relationship to the deceased. He normally is given a pig or shotgun by the eldest male of the enemy family. Often the younger members of the respective families wish to pursue the feud, but the two elders (*untä*), arriving at the negotiated settlement, inform them that the fighting is ended. The man receiving payment would consider it a personal offense if one of the members of his family ignored the settlement.

Feuds also sometimes end simply when one of the eldest men on one side is killed. Such a person is normally the father or father-in-law of the men in his family. Such a killing of an *untä* normally concludes the feud, the final killers having "won."

On occasion, a feud is of short duration, lasting only until each group of kinsmen has lost a man. The final killers then may send the message, "Let us stop killing. Now all is paid because you have killed and we have killed." There are no rituals ever involved in terminating hostilities.

War

"War," in the Jívaro meaning, is conducted not to wreak vengeance upon any particular individual, but to secure as many human heads as possible from an alien tribe, usually the Achuara. This purpose contrasts distinctly with the revenge killing of a specific individual in the same tribe which characterizes feuding. A less emphasized war objective is to capture women. No case could be found of war being pursued to seize territory.

There is a "gray" area in which the patterns of feuding and war overlap to a limited degree. This seems to be a reflection of such factors as the absence of a tribal political structure, the intermittent escalation of intra-tribal feuding, and the relative isolation of many neighborhoods from one another. Thus, while full-fledged head-taking raids are only launched against other groups "that speak differently," i.e., have different dialects or languages, such as the Achuara, the assassination of a man belonging to a very distant neighborhood within the tribe may be followed occasionally by the taking of his head or by taking hair from his head to make a *tsantsa* with a tree gourd (see pp. 147–48). The latter type of *tsantsa* may also be made with the hair of a victim from a closer neighborhood provided that enmity towards its population is extremely strong in the killer's own locality.

A war or head-taking raid is organized by a man who is a *kakaram*, and who has previously killed at least three or four persons.[2] When the *kakaram* decides to lead a raid, he asks an *untä* of his neighborhood, ideally a respected, elderly man who has also killed at least several times, to be the *wea*, or master of ceremonies, for the first celebration when the raiding party returns. If he agrees, the *kakaram* and some of the expected participants in the expedition build the *wea* a new, large house for the feast, the construction work usually taking some months.

When the house is finished, and about two weeks before the planned expedition, the organizer sends spies to the Achuara neighborhood he plans to attack in order to select the most likely house(s) for assault. Then he sends a son or son-in-law as a "recruiter" to visit other neighborhoods to invite men to join the expedition. The recruiter personally visits every house where he thinks he may find a willing participant. When he arrives in a new neighborhood, he first visits the house of a known friendly relative. The latter acts as his protector and takes him to visit every likely household in the locality. Then, if there are adjacent neighborhoods where the relative has a friendly kinsman but the recruiter does not, the relative may send a son along with him to protect and introduce him to potential recruits. In this manner, a recruiter can canvass a dozen neighborhoods, although generally the number is only half that many. When the recruiter reaches the most distant neighborhood and prepares to return home, he sends a new recruit ahead on the return trail to notify the people of the next neighborhood to prepare for the arrival of the war party. The men of the next neighborhood thus have time to get ready to leave on the expedition, and also the women can prepare food and beer for the arriving group. The other neighborhoods along the route are similarly notified as the expedition progresses. Finally, all members of the war party, normally numbering about thirty or forty, arrive at the house of the *wea*. As each enters the house, he engages in a ritualistic shouting chant (*enermartin*) with the *wea*. During the chanting each man stamps back and forth in turn, thrusting his shotgun in rhythm, as though threatening the other speaker. This chant, which primarily focuses on establishing the identity and demonstrating the supernatural power of the speakers, is also used when complete strangers happen to encounter one another on a trail.[3]

The party may spend two to four days at the house, preparing rations for the trail. On the day of departure, they wake a few hours before dawn, form two lines and perform the chant simultaneously until close to daybreak. Then they drink from jars of beer placed before them, and the *wea* declares, "I am very hungry. Bring me plenty of fish." This is a metaphorical allusion to the Achuara, who subsist on fish much more than the Jívaro, and to the *tsantsa* which are to be brought back wrapped up in cloth, much as fish are brought from the river wrapped in moist leaves to keep them fresh.

The *kakaram* warrior sponsoring the raid is usually the expedition leader or chief. There is no special title for this role, beyond the usual *untä*. There may be two war chiefs if the neighborhood that has the biggest representation in the expedition is one other than the sponsor's. The war leader(s) is theoretically expected to be strictly obeyed by the other members of the party, but only for the duration of the expedition, while it is in hostile territory.

Obedience, even on a war expedition, is often not as rigorous in practice as it is in theory. Any member of the party who tells the war leader that he has "dreamed badly" and therefore would like to avoid participating in the attack, is invariably excused from such participation. In the actual attack, some of the inexperienced and less aggressive warriors are backed up by a few *kakaram* who encourage their advance forward.

Since the war expedition is normally composed of men from a number of neighborhoods, some of whom are bound to be enemies of others, the members of the party tend to be organized into a "buddy system" in which pairs of close relatives "cover" one another from assassination by another expedition member. In this manner, it is possible to organize a large force despite the fact that many of its members may be enemies. This system has undoubtedly contributed to the ability of the Jívaro to ally against outside invaders in the past.

With the entrance of the raiding group into the alien tribe's region, strict silence is maintained and scouts are sent ahead. The latter, usually five in number, snake back and forth through the forest across the trail, to avoid being surprised by Achuara hostiles. The main body of men follows the scouts, but simply keeps to the trail itself.

At nightfall, the entire party stops, while the scouts remain awake, camped at an outpost on the trail ahead. The main body constructs lean-to's and sleeps, except for one man who is sent several hundred yards ahead to act as a sentry until about 1 A.M., when he returns. Then the main group arises at about 2 or 3 A.M., eats, and continues on the trail. When they reach the scout outpost, the scouts are relieved by a new group which proceeds on ahead of the main body. The former scouts go back down the trail to sleep in the lean-to's where the main party had spent the night.

The actual attack is carried out only on a house where the scouts find the enemy unwarned. Usually a single house is attacked, but sometimes two may be assaulted simultaneously, and the attackers may use palm-wood thrusting lances, bayonet-style, to supplement their muzzle-loaders. Often the roof of the house is set afire to drive the inhabitants out into the open. Heads are taken of all victims, regardless of age or sex. A man may seize an Achuara girl or woman as a captive to try to take her home to be an extra wife, but usually he is unsuccessful in this because one of his companions kills her on the homeward trail to secure a head trophy.

The capture of women sometimes goes in the other direction, and can involve children as well. A male informant recounted that when he was a small child, the Huambisa attacked his house in the Río Yaupi region, killed his father, and captured his mother and himself. After several years in their captor's household, they escaped and, after an arduous journey, reached their home neighborhood. However, most wife-seizing among the Jívaro is intra-, rather than inter-tribal in form, and is often justified on the basis of supposed levirate rights and romantic involvement

Although obtaining heads is the primary objective of the expedition, the successful attackers also loot the houses of such valuables as blowguns, dart poison, dogs, beads, machetes, steel axes, featherwork, and other ornaments.

Tsantsa *Celebrations*

As they retreat homeward, the head-takers (*tsaŋram*) shrink the skins peeled from the heads. Since the withdrawal from the enemy region is made with haste, in order to avoid being overtaken by an avenging group of Achuara, the preparation of the head skins is done intermittently during the infrequent stops on the return.

The process of preparing the *tsantsa* involves a number of steps. With the aid of a machete or steel knife, the victim's skin is peeled back from the uppermost part of his chest, shoulders and back, and the head and neck are cut off as close as possible to the collarbone. The killer removes his own woven headband or *etsemat* and passes it through the mouth and neck of the head and ties it over his shoulder to facilitate his rapid retreat from the victim's neighborhood. If he has no *etsemat*, he may use a section of *činčipï* vine instead.

Eventually, the head-taker and his companions reach a spot beside a river where they had cached one or more pottery cooking jars and food dishes. Here he makes a slit up the rear of the head, carefully cuts the skin from the skull, and throws the latter into the river "as a gift for *paŋi*," the anaconda. The skin is boiled in plain water (there are no "secret" vegetal additives) for no more than about half an hour (otherwise "the hair would fall out"). The skin, already reduced perhaps by half, is lifted out with a stick which is then thrust into the ground so that the trophy will dry. Then the skin is turned inside out and all the flesh adhering to it is scraped off with a knife. The scraped skin is turned right side out and the slit in the rear is sewn together with string made from the inner bark of the *kumai* palm. A vine is also sewn around the inside of the base of the neck and the lips are tied with the same kind of string.

Five or six stones about two inches in diameter are heated in the fire. Each, in turn, is lifted with a four-pronged stick into the "sack" formed by the head skin and rolled around inside. When the stone cools, the head-taker grasps the *tsantsa* by the hair in order to turn it over to drop the stone back into the fire. When the skin is too small for pebbles to be rolled around in it, sand is heated in the food bowl and substituted for the pebbles, the inverted *tsantsa* being covered with a large leaf to keep in the heat. Periodically, the head-taker massages the skin to help the drying process and to affect the shape. The vine around the base of the neck is gradually drawn in closer so that the neck will become reduced in proportion to the head. After about an hour of this additional work with the heated sand, the expedition resumes its running trip homeward, stopping every afternoon for about two or three hours to continue the hot sand treatment of the skins. In addition, a machete is heated red-hot and pressed against the lips to dry them. Then three chonta palm pins are put through the lips and are lashed together with string of the *kumai* inner bark. The skin is also rubbed daily with finely powdered balsa wood charcoal so that it will become blackened and thus prevent the *muisak* of the murdered man from seeing out (see pp. 143–46). A large, hard red seed sometimes is also placed under each eyelid, filling any slight aperture which may remain.

A total of approximately six days of such intermittent preparation is normally involved in the preparation of the *tsantsa* until it is its final size, slightly larger than a man's fist. The last day of work on the trophy is usually spent in the forest within a few hours' walk from the neighborhood where the first *tsantsa* celebration or feast will take place. So that the head-taker will be able to hang the *tsantsa* from his neck in the celebration, a hole is made in the top of the head and a doubled *kumai* bark string is inserted and tied to a short stick of chonta palm on the inside.

When the war party arrives at the neighborhood from which they departed, they do not go directly to the *wea*'s house but rather to the home of a nearby neighbor. A young man is sent to advise the *wea* that "now we are coming with plenty of dried fish," alluding to the heads of the Achuara. The *wea* then sends him and others to inform households in his own and adjacent neighborhoods of the victory and to tell them to come in two days to attend the first *tsantsa* celebration (*numpeŋ*) which is held at the newly built house of the *wea*.

The *wea* also immediately goes to visit the war party at the neighbor's house. Each head-taker holds up his *tsantsa*, wrapped in cloth "to keep the hair in place," for inspection by the *wea*, who parts the fabric, bends down and smells each one, saying, "It is delicious fish. It has an excellent smell." After having thus inspected the results of the raid, the *wea* returns home. In two days, the war party follows, is joined at the *wea*'s house by their relatives and neighbors, and all participate together in a brief, two day, version of the *tsantsa* celebration (see pp. 146–47) for the basic religious ideas involved in this and the subsequent feasts).

When this first *tsantsa* feast is concluded, the head-takers return to their separate homes and begin to make preparations for the two subsequent feasts which each of them will host individually. Since enormous quantities of beer and food are consumed at these celebrations, the head-taker normally has to clear additional garden space for his wife or wives to plant to assure an ample supply of manioc. The first of these two celebrations, named *suamak*, normally takes place no sooner than after a year, to allow time for garden clearing and the growth of a large mature crop of manioc as well as for the raising of pigs to help provide meat for the feasting. Also the host may delay the celebration in order to build a new, larger house more worthy of the occasion. Thus, often two or three years pass before a man gives the feast.

To assure a large quantity of wild game for the feast, men who are close relatives of the host separately go hunting long distances from the house for a period of approximately nine or ten days before the opening day. Lacking any mnemonic system for keeping count of the days accurately, they are able to time their return to coincide with the arrival of the guests at the feast with the aid of an ingenious device which might be called a "banana clock." That is, the host gives each hunter a green cooking banana or plantain from the same stalk, which is one of those hanging in the house to ripen for the feast. When each of the hunters' plantains is almost fully ripe, they know that it is time to return for the celebration. The host also sends or delivers plantains from the same stalk to those invited guests living at some distance so that they, too, will arrive at the same time.

The celebration lasts five days and is followed, about a month later, by the third feast (*napiŋ*). This is the largest of all, with the head-taker supplying food and drink for six days. He must be able to provide plentifully for all his guests or the occasion would cause him to lose, rather than to gain, prestige. Guests at the feasts usually number up to about 125–150 persons, and mainly come from the local neighborhoods. Since these last two feasts, totaling eleven days of unremitted hospitality, must be supplied from the same harvest, often little food remains in the gardens at the end of the celebrations. Not uncommonly, the host and his family are forced onto a relatively meager diet for some months thereafter until the gardens can recover from their near-exhaustion. Sometimes such a large amount of the gardens' supply of manioc is consumed that the host is unable to follow the second feast with the third. There is no stigma attached to this, but it means that the *tsantsa* never undergoes its final modification.

When, and if, all three feasts have been given, the chonta pins and palm-fiber string are removed from the mouth of the *tsantsa* and replaced with long white cotton strings (see Plate 21). The reason given for not using cotton strings during the shrinking stage is that they would have burned. The strings, two to each of the three lip holes, are intertwined near the mouth and dangle below as much as a yard, transected by three horizontal red bands of achiote paint. Often miniature ear ornaments of red and yellow toucan breast feathers are also hung from the ears at this time, the most correctly made examples having three such pendants from each lobe. In this finished form, the *tsantsa* may be kept as a decorative keepsake in the house for years. It may be worn by the head-taker on solitary, meditative walks in the forest, or in social dances at his house, and, if not eventually traded to the whites, it may finally be buried with him.[4]

The primary purpose of the *tsantsa* feast, from the Jívaro point of view, is not supernatural, although that is recognized by them as a secondary purpose; but is to acquire prestige, friendship, and obligations through being recognized as an accomplished warrior and, through the feasting, by being a generous host to as many neighbors as possible. One informant observed, "The desire of the Jívaro for heads is like the desire of the whites for gold."

Since the head-taking raids are directed at the Achuara and others "who live far away," the victim whose head is the focal point of the celebration normally is viewed by everyone in the head-taker's neighborhood as an "enemy." Accordingly, it is the unique occasion for the members of many Jívaro households to get together to reaffirm their common identity and unity. Under such circumstances, it is not surprising that the *tsantsa* feast is participated in with great joy and a cumulative sense of euphoria. Of course, the huge quantities of strong manioc beer help, as do the ritual circle dances (*wainči*), which continue from dusk to dawn night after night. The bountiful quantities of meat and garden foods add to the sense of well-being. It is also a time of relative sexual license, as I had occasion to observe during the one *tsantsa* feast that I attended. Liaisons are arranged discreetly by both unmarried and married individuals, who rendezvous in the forest surrounding the house.

The supernatural and ritual aspects of the celebration contribute to the sense of solidarity by inhibiting fights between men who have become drunk and who may try to even a score with old enemies or with men who have offended them at the feast by flirting with their wives. That is, it is believed that the avenging soul (*muisak*) of the murdered man will be able to take advantage of any disruption of the binding ritual by escaping from the *tsantsa* to cause an ongoing fight to culminate in a death. Permitting the *muisak* to escape from the *tsantsa* would also be an affront to the host, since it would negate the major supernatural purpose of the feast, that is, to utilize the power of the *muisak*, while it is resident in the

tsantsa, for increasing the power of women who are members
of the host's household. Therefore, any fight that erupts is
immediately stopped by the other male participants, led by
the male master of ceremonies, the *wea,* who usually has been
selected for the role because of his considerable ritual knowledge and prestige. Fights between females at the feast, although less common, are similarly halted by the women, led
by the female ceremonial leader, the *uhá,* who is selected on a
basis similar to that for the *wea.* Thus the religious, ritual,
and social pressures of the occasion operate to make it the
safest, most euphoric, and largest social gathering known to
the Jívaro. It is not surprising, therefore, that the *tsantsa*
feasts tend to be viewed by the Jívaro as the pinnacles of
their social lives. It is also expectable, given the ethos of killing and counter-killing, that this, the greatest celebration,
centers around the indisputable evidence of a triumph over a
common enemy. The intimate interaction between the euphoria of the celebration and the awareness of the murdered
enemy is illustrated by this *tsantsa* feast circle dance song:

> Today, today, let us greet the dawn only playing.
> Today, today, let us greet the dawn only playing.
> Chuwi[5] tells me,
> Chuwi tells me
> We are going to greet the dawn playing.
> Chuwi tells me,
> Chuwi tells me
> We are going to greet the dawn.
>
> And they taught me previously,
> I cannot sleep easily,
> And I will meet the dawn together with Chuwi.
> And don't you sleep!
> And don't you sleep!
> For now it is dawning, for now it is dawning.

Chapter VI

CULTURAL CHANGE

Information on cultural change among the interior Jívaro
was obtained exclusively from elderly informants, a method
which was necessitated by the lack of written records. By
employing such time markers as the appearance of Halley's
Comet (1910),[1] the end of visits by rubber collectors (ca.
1914–15), and the dates of the founding of various missions
among the frontier Jívaro, of which the interior Jívaro were
aware, approximate indications were obtained of the inception
and duration of many of the changes. Such information usually consisted of reports of trends rather than of abrupt
alterations in native cultural practices, the isolation of the
interior area having protected the Jívaro there from the dis-
ruptive incursions of the gold miners, missionaries, and settlers to the west.

In the absence of adequate historical documentation, in-
terviewing techniques were used which had already been
developed in "salvage" or "memory" ethnography among
North American Indians. Using such techniques, anthropologists in such areas as California had succeeded in making
very useful reconstructions of bygone aboriginal cultures with
no more than a few aged informants as their source of
information. In the Jívaro case, the task was much easier, in
that there was still a fully functioning native culture and a
variety of good informants whose accounts could be compared in determining what changes had occurred during their
lifetimes.

To check the reliability of the oral accounts of cultural

changes, the investigator normally attempted to compare the views of a number of persons regarding modifications in each type of cultural activity. Accordingly, a trend is reported here only if it was substantiated independently by at least several reliable informants. To heighten the accuracy of such information, the trends reported here are further restricted to those which the informants had observed during the passage of their own lifetimes. Changes that had reportedly gone on in the culture previously, and for which the information was therefore of a hearsay type, are not included unless specifically so noted. Thus the reported changes primarily occurred during the period ca. 1895–1957. The ethnographic present in this chapter, as elsewhere, is 1956–57.

It should be pointed out that the material that follows often includes consideration of causal factors from the informants' point of view. Such statements of opinion regarding causal relationships between changes are, unless otherwise indicated, those of elderly, knowledgeable informants whom I respected for their intelligence and ability to analyze the events about them. In asking and respecting the opinions of native informants about causality I depart from the position of some anthropologists who have seemed to doubt the ability of non-literate peoples to provide meaningful analysis of causal relationships within their own culture. On the contrary, I have found that the Jívaro are extremely aware of, and alert to, the factors directly influencing their lives; and normally I found their hypotheses superior to those that I proposed and tested in the field. Unlike some other non-literate populations, for example the Conibo Indians of eastern Peru, whom I have also studied, the Jívaro almost never explain any behavior, traditional or otherwise, on the basis of such a statement as "we do it that way because our ancestors did" or "we do it that way because other people would laugh at us if we did it differently." The Jívaro seem proud of their ability to judge for themselves the usefulness of continuing or changing their traditional behavior on very pragmatic and personal grounds. All this does not mean to convey the idea that the Jívaro are natural anthropologists, but simply that their knowledge of the factors which influence the changes that they make as individuals should be respected sufficiently to be collected and included as useful ethnological data.

The main variables introduced into interior Jívaro culture during the period studied were Western-manufactured trade goods, especially machetes, axes, and guns. Some machetes were acquired by the frontier Jívaro near Macas about a hundred years ago,[2] but very few reached the interior Jívaro by intra-tribal trade until the turn of the century, and even these were so scarce and valued that their blades were each split into fragments to permit their utilization by several households. The more efficient steel blade fragments were at first used in the same manner as the aboriginal stone axe heads, each machete piece being mounted into a wooden handle. After the 1930's, however, machetes became sufficiently abundant so that the need to split the blades into small fragments was eliminated. They also largely replaced by then the traditional palm-wood "machetes" used in cutting down garden weeds. Despite their fair degree of availability at the present time, steel machetes are still highly valued and are used for many years, long after they have lost their handles and have become worn down to a fraction of their former size. Today they are considered to be utterly indispensable tools by the Jívaro, who also have been able to acquire some single-bitted steel axe-heads, although in much smaller numbers than the machetes.

The introduction of machetes and steel axes has made woodworking and tree felling more efficient and rapid. The formerly tedious work of felling trees for garden clearings with the aboriginal stone axes has been described by Up de Graff for the Jivaroan "Antipas" (a neighborhood of the Aguaruna or Huambisa) among whom he resided in the late nineteenth century:

If you saw the one-handed stone axes which are the only tools these people have with which to fell the enormous trees, many of them three to five feet in diameter, to make their clearings (often five acres in extent), you would wonder how it were possible to accomplish this feat. It is a feat of patience rather than of skill. The wood is not cut, but reduced to a pulp, six or eight men working round one tree at the same time.

The first step in making a *chacra* [Spanish: garden] is to remove the undergrowth; the soft stems are cut with hardwood machetes, what can be torn up by the roots is torn up, and the small saplings are snapped off by main force. Then the attention of the workers is turned to the larger trees. A ring is cut round the trunks of all the trees within a radius of, say, a hundred feet of some picked giant, enough to weaken them, and prepare them for the final strain which breaks them off. Finally the giant itself is attacked by a party with axes which works *for days and weeks* [emphasis supplied], until at last there comes a day when the great trunk has been eaten away sufficiently for it to crack and fall. But it does not fall alone, for it drags with it all the smaller trees in its vicinity which are bound to it and to one another by an unbreakable network of creepers among the upper branches . . .

After leaving the trees to lie for several months during the dry season, the Antipas fire them, a process which eliminates all the smaller limbs and bush, leaving only the trunks, to deal with which they have no tools. I have examined the stumps of these fallen trees many a time; they resemble in every respect those of a clearing made by beavers.[3]

Today such "giant" trees as referred to by Up de Graff are often felled in a matter of hours by a single man employing a steel axe, or somewhat longer if he only has a machete.

Despite the increased availability of steel axes and machetes for land clearing and weeding in recent decades, the size of forest areas cleared for gardens has not become larger. In fact, garden size and agricultural production are actually reported to have decreased by perhaps a third of what they were several decades ago.[4] Specifically, elderly informants estimate that the present garden size per nuclear family is one half to three quarters of what it was in 1925. They attribute the decline in agricultural production to the disinclination of the young men to clear land "because they do not like to work hard the way their fathers did." Instead, according to the informants, the younger men have their minds fixed on acquiring shotguns, steel tools, and other goods by becoming shamans or trading partners, and also spend more time than formerly in visiting each other's houses, drinking, and engaging in pre- and extra-marital sexual adventures.

There has also been a growing tendency for each household to have several small garden plots rather than the single large garden which was previously typical. This change is attributed to the fact that the steel axe and machete are so much more efficient than the preceding stone tools that a man can now successfully work alone in tree felling without needing to call on his neighbors for help. By avoiding asking them for help, he hopes to maintain better relations with them and thereby secure their services in some more important matter. Since a man usually works alone at intermittent times, the individual garden plots tend to be smaller than those resulting from a large sustained effort by a group of neighbors.

Within the household, the basic aspects of life seem little changed except with regard to the amount of time men spend in land clearing and weaving. In recent decades, the time spent on these activities has been reduced, respectively, by the adoption of steel cutting tools and the acquisition of Western and Achuara cloth and articles of dress through trading partnerships. A man instead spends a larger percentage of his time simply relaxing in the house, going hunting to obtain skins for trade, and visiting other households.

The period of temporary matrilocal residence has become shortened in recent decades so that it now usually ends soon after the birth of the first child. Formerly, the couple commonly remained in the wife's parents' house until after the birth of the second or third child. The factors behind this change are not clear except that some informants said that in-laws were not getting along as well as they used to do in the old days. The occasional practice of avoiding temporary matrilocal residence and bride-service, by giving the bride's father a shotgun, is reportedly a recent development.

The introduction of firearms, starting slowly at about the turn of the century, constituted a major technological change in Jívaro culture comparable in importance to the adoption of steel cutting tools. At that time, during the height of the Amazon rubber boom, a few Winchester .44 caliber carbines were acquired by the interior Jívaro from the Achuara, the firearms being captured during head-taking raids. The acquisition of great numbers of firearms by the interior Jívaro, however, is a development of only the last three decades. The new firearms, which are muzzle-loading shotguns of Spanish manufacture, and possessed by virtually every adult male, have been acquired along with gunpowder and shot by trade from the frontier Jívaro. These firearms are still being obtained in ever greater numbers.

The development of long-distance chains of trading partners between the interior Jívaro and adjacent tribes is an especially noteworthy change, mainly occurring since the end of the Amazon rubber boom, about 1914–15. The impetus for this development was provided by the fact that the end of the rubber boom found the Achuara tribe, which had been much more involved in the rubber trade than the Jívaro, suddenly cut off from their supply of firearms and ammunition. At the same time, trade between the frontier Jívaro and the whites at Macas and Méndez was beginning to develop significantly, and the Jívaro also wanted Achuara products, particularly blowguns and dart poison. The essential result was that both the Jívaro and the Achuara found it profitable to develop mutual trade. To the former inventory of products traded within the Jívaro tribe, such as salt and machete blade fragments, were added new goods coming from the frontier Jívaro on the west, and the Achuara in the east. The new goods primarily have been firearms, gunpowder, increased quantities of steel cutting tools from the frontier Jívaro, and featherwork, blowguns, and dart poison from the Achuara.

In connection with trading partnerships, a minor ritual has been learned from the Achuara tribe. This is the ceremony in which two men embrace each other, kneeling on a cloth, to formalize a partnership relationship. Previously any contractual ritual was unknown.

The now universal demand among the interior Jívaro for firearms and gunpowder has made the men of every neighborhood extremely dependent on those persons who have trading partners in neighborhoods nearer the regions of white settlement in the west. The intensification of the trading partnership pattern in recent decades has also been associated with the more common use of the "friend" term of address (*amiči*) between people in general, in preference to kinship terms. The "friend" term is now used increasingly: (1) to remind neighbors and relatives subtly of some earlier obligation; and (2) to indicate a friendly feeling for the person addressed beyond the necessities of kinship obligations.

The only discernible changes in kinship formal structure have occurred in the adoption, increase, or decrease in use of a few specific terms of address by men and the adoption of a men's term of reference (*awe*) by women. A few Achuara terms of address have been introduced through the inter-tribal trading partnerships. These are indicated on Table 1, which shows also the elementary kinship terms of reference and the terms of address.

One of the clearest socio-economic trends has been the tendency for ever greater numbers of persons, especially men, to become shamans, as well as trading partners, during the past few decades. Informants uniformly ascribe this trend to the desire of individuals to acquire "white men's valuables," especially machetes and firearms, and to distribute these goods in order to win friendship. The considerable growth of socio-economic power wielded by shamans in their neighborhoods is also a recent development involving: (1) an increase in their proportionate numbers in the population; (2) a growth in the demand for their services; and (3) an increase in their accumulated material valuables, with the resulting development of some individual differentiation in terms of wealth in trade goods. This development has been facilitated by the fact that the shamans can successfully accumulate goods because of the laymen's fear of asking them for gifts. The rise in numbers of shamans is also believed to have increased the amount of illness and death due to witchcraft.

Shaman hierarchies within the neighborhood are also an important new development. This innovation, which is related to the growth in numbers of shamans competing to acquire valuables and strong shamanistic power, occurred between about 1925 and 1935. Formerly, only one shaman normally was found in each neighborhood, but with the increase in their numbers, they began to purchase their power from other shamans within their own localities, thereby bringing into existence hierarchies of shaman partners on the neighborhood level.

The inter-neighborhood hierarchies of shamans linking the Jívaro with the Canelos are likewise a new development, evolving since about 1930. According to older informants, shamanistic power formerly was not obtained from the Canelos tribe, but with the inhibition of inter-tribal warfare, Jívaro shamans began to visit the Canelos shamans, leading to the elaborate hierarchical relations which now stretch northward to the Canelos "banks." The increasing competition between Jívaro shamans, deriving from their sheer numbers and their demand for trade goods, further encouraged them to travel northward to get the maximum quality and variety of *tsentsak* available.

Shamanistic knowledge and practices have experienced considerable elaboration in recent decades. Much of this more elaborate knowledge has been learned from the Canelos tribe via the inter-tribal system of shaman hierarchies. Examples of such recently transmitted information include new types of spirit helpers and the innovation of possession by spirits of the dead. The heightened shamanistic competition has encouraged the acquisition of new techniques and knowledge.

Outside of shamanism, few changes have occurred in supernatural ideology. Some minor modifications have occurred in the case of techniques used to obtain *arutam* souls. First, a former method of encountering *arutam* has virtually disappeared. It involved walking a specially prepared straight and wide trail alone at night armed only with a wooden shield and magical staff. The disappearance of this technique is ascribed to the abandonment of wooden shields as a functional item of warfare following the adoption of firearms. Second, *Banisteriopsis*, as opposed to *Datura*, has become less commonly used to see *arutam*, a change attributed to the fact that the increasingly numerous shamans have been using up the available supply of *Banisteriopsis*. Furthermore, because of the shortage of *Banisteriopsis*, families tend to reserve the known vines (wild or cultivated) for use by shamans when they come to cure family members believed to be suffering from bewitching.

A very few individuals among the interior Jívaro are beginning to consider the possibility that the "true" or "ordinary" souls (*nekás wakaní*) may go to the interior of the active volcano Sangay at a person's death, a belief transmitted from the frontier Jívaro, who learned the idea from Catholic missionaries. The latter use the volcano's name in Jívaro, Tuŋurä, as a synonym for Hell. This was one of the few ideological items among the interior Jívaro clearly ascribable to Western cultural influence.

A strong rise in interpersonal offenses and the application of retaliatory sanctions is reported for the past four or five decades. The increase is particularly strong in the cases of adultery and murder by means of witchcraft, physical violence, and poisoning. The increase in shamanistically induced murders is primarily attributed to the growth in numbers of shamans attempting to accumulate wealth in the form of "white man's valuables." The rise in murders or assassinations through shooting or poisoning is seen by the Jívaro partially as a retaliatory response to the growth in fatal be-witchings.

The rise in adultery is attributed to the tendency of young men not to work as hard as in former decades and instead to spend their time visiting other households to drink beer, look for sexual partners, and perhaps obtain trade goods through making "friends." This increase in intra-neighborhood visiting and shamanism may be due to the greater leisure time available for the men since the introduction of steel cutting tools, but informants themselves primarily ascribe the trends in visiting and shamanism to the young men's fixation on the acquisition of the "white man's valuables," particularly firearms, and a resultant de-emphasis on hard physical work, especially in land clearing.

The growth in witchcraft, and of the sanctions applied against it, has resulted in an intensification of the traditional Jívaro feuding pattern during the past half-century. The Jívaro partially ascribe this intensification to the decline of inter-tribal head-taking raids which they themselves recognize as having been an activity which acted as an outlet for men who wished to engage in killing. Today, because of the trade-derived inhibitions against raids on the Achuara, killings and protracted feuding have become more frequent within the Jívaro tribe and even within the neighborhood.

Inter-tribal head-taking raids, i.e., "war," in contrast, have declined steadily both in frequency and size for about the last four to five decades. Today usually not more than one such expedition takes place every year, and a war party rarely exceeds forty warriors, whereas at the turn of the century such expeditions apparently were almost monthly attacking the Achuara, and an estimated four hundred to five hundred warriors sometimes took part in a single raid.

The decline in inter-tribal warfare is attributed to the

growth of inter-tribal trading partnerships, whose participants and their relatives have a vested interest in the maintenance of inter-tribal peace to protect the partners. Relatives
of the traders threaten to apply sanctions against their own
tribesmen if they should initiate war against the Achuara. The
Achuara, who have the same interest in maintaining the trading system, similarly discourage inter-tribal raids against the
Jívaro.

Winchesters and shotguns have almost entirely replaced
palm-wood thrusting lances as the chief combat weapons
both for offense and defense. Formerly, spears thrown with
the spear-thrower were used along with thrusting lances in
attacks, while poisoned blowgun darts and double-pointed
palm throwing sticks were used in household defense, the
latter being cast from now vanished house towers. Round
wooden shields, formerly universally carried in combat, are
likewise no longer used in fighting, due to their inadequacy
against guns. The use of shields is now restricted to rare
ritual functions, especially in the *tsantsa* feast. Such ceremonial feasts have considerably diminished in size and frequency
as a consequence of the decline in inter-tribal head-taking
raids.

Changes in house construction during the past few decades have been influenced primarily by the adoption of firearms for fighting. Formerly, the roof of the house was
sometimes surmounted by a wooden defensive tower from
which missiles could be showered onto attackers. Today such
towers have entirely disappeared, since the use of guns by
attackers only made the position of defenders in the towers
untenable.

At the same time, the use of firearms has encouraged
the construction of breastworks of horizontally placed logs
inside of house walls as a protection against gunfire. The

digging of foxholes in house floors is a related new development. The construction of double walls behind beds has become common to protect sleepers from assassins attempting to shoot between the palm staves of the house wall at night. The construction of escape tunnels has declined considerably since the lessening of inter-tribal warfare, for their prime function was to provide a means of escaping the wholesale attacks and sieges which only occur in the inter-tribal head-taking raids. Log signal drums are now also relatively rare, due to the adoption of firearms, whose discharge is sufficient in itself to alert neighbors when an attack occurs.

A decline has occurred in the last three or four decades in the numbers of pigs kept, which is ascribed primarily to the fact that *tsantsa* feasts now have become much less frequent due to the lessening of inter-tribal warfare. The raising of pigs was primarily directed towards having a large supply of meat for such feasts. The capturing and taming of wild animals and birds has increased, however, because of the demand for these by Jívaro trading partners to the west, who trade them to the whites of the frontier.

Hunting has become more important as an activity to procure skins and feathers for trade, although there is no indication that such specialized hunting has resulted in an increase of meat consumption in the household. The adoption of firearms has tended to increase the hunters' efficiency in killing rare birds, such as the toucan, which are prized for their plumage and are difficult to stalk at close range. Firearms also have facilitated the hunting of dangerous wild animals for their skins, especially the jaguar and peccary, which were formerly hunted with the lance.

Besides firearms, blowguns and curare dart poison are also utilized for hunting to a greater degree than was the case several decades ago. The intensified use of blowguns has been made possible by the development of trade with the Achuara, who are the main regional producers of blowguns and curare. Formerly, blowguns and curare could only be obtained in small quantities by looting Achuara houses after a successful head-hunting raid.

In the case of fishing, no noticeable trends have occurred except for a very minor increase in the use of hook-and-line technique due to the acquisition of some steel fish hooks by means of the inter-tribal trade network.

Wild food gathering has been marked by a decline in the collection of the formerly important chonta palm fruit. This decline in collection, interestingly enough, is attributed to the introduction of the steel machete, whose efficiency, compared to the stone axe, made it easy for men to chop down chonta palms simply for their edible tips, thereby reducing the number of trees available as regular sources of the hanging clusters of fruit. In other words, the introduction of steel cutting tools, by contributing to the degradation of this wild food resource, decreased rather than increased food obtained from gathering.

Species of domesticated plants remain unchanged except for two new additions, *papa china* and the onion, introduced by means of trading partners from the frontier Jívaro, who in turn had adopted them from the missionaries and Ecuadorian settlers. None of the aboriginal native crops has been abandoned within the memory of the informants.

The sexual division of labor in agricultural activities is unchanged except for the relatively inconsequential harvesting of the small plantings of red pepper and sugar cane. Formerly, both sexes engaged in harvesting these, whereas now only women do. The decline of male interest in harvesting sugar cane seems to be due to the fact that since the adoption of firearms, blowguns and poisoned darts are rarely used any more in defending houses against attack. Sugar cane was the chief antidote against the curare dart poison, and men going on a killing expedition would carry some to suck on if hit by a dart.

Despite the efficiency of the steel tools and their increased supply, the quantity and quality of the artifacts produced through their use does not seem to have particularly changed. In other aspects of work, the machete has replaced the aboriginal bamboo knife for skinning animals and cutting meat, and has almost entirely taken the place of the palm-wood "machete" in clearing gardens of weeds. Steel needles obtained from the West have partially replaced bone ones for sewing and boring. The traditional bone needles, because of their large size, are still preferred for some tasks, especially the making of netted bags. A new minor craft is the fashioning of powder horns from unworked cow horns obtained from trading partners in the west, who secure them from the whites.

The preparation of animal skins for trade has increased considerably in order to acquire steel tools, shotguns, and gunpowder from the frontier Jívaro trading partners. Cordage manufacture remains unchanged, but the local production of knotted and knotless netting bags is a new development, learned from the Achuara tribe as a result of the increased peaceful contacts by trading partners.

Western-manufactured clothing, along with trade cloth and glass beads, has been adopted gradually by men and women as a result of the development of the trading partnership system. The increased trade has also resulted in the acquisition of Achuara-woven cotton kilts. The acquisition of both Western and Achuara items of dress has greatly contributed to a decline in the home weaving of garments by Jívaro. Bark clothing, viewed as a sign of poverty, has become less common than in former times, this change also being attributed to the growing supply of clothing and cloth obtained through trading partners.

Feather headdresses and bird skins are prepared in larger quantities than in previous decades, a trend ascribed to the increasing demand for these items for trade to the frontier Jívaro in exchange for firearms and machetes. Featherwork of Achuara origin is also more plentiful, and some of it is traded on to the frontier Jívaro in the west.

In summation, it can be said that the technological introductions, especially steel cutting tools and firearms, have become the most desired valuables among the interior Jívaro because of their great efficiency compared to the aboriginal equivalents. They have been put to the same basic exchange uses as traditional Jívaro valuables such as featherwork, i.e., they have been used as gifts to acquire services and reinforce obligations. However, the great demand for these new, highly valued goods has made them more significant instruments for attaining social ends, and the creative changes which have occurred in the culture following these introductions appear to be primarily connected to the acquisition, accumulation and distribution of the new items as valuables. Such developments have included the rise of intra- and inter-tribal trading partnerships, the growth in numbers of shamans, and the creation of intra- and inter-tribal shaman hierarchies. Through these developments, the technological introductions also may have indirectly contributed to the decline in inter-tribal warfare and to the reported increase in intra-tribal witchcraft and feuding. The total effect of the new technology on food production seems quite uncertain, with wild-plant gathering, pig-raising, and agriculture apparently showing declines, the latter two since at least about 1925.

EPILOGUE

In the summer of 1969 I revisited the *untsuri šuarä* both east and west of the Cordillera de Cutucú. The changes in Jívaro life that had occurred, even since my last fieldwork in 1964, were far more extensive than anything I could have predicted. Small airstrips, primarily opened up by the missionaries, now dot almost all of the Jívaro region. Under missionary sponsorship, bilingual Jívaro schoolteachers have been placed in the most remote locations, and medical treatment is periodically dispensed along with evangelization.

Ecuadorian army garrisons are now found in the *untsuri šuarä* territory as far east as the Río Pangui, where there is now a major air-supplied military base and Salesian mission (Taisha), as well as a new settlement of more than one hundred white colonists. Missionaries have collaborated with the military and police forces both west and east of the Cutucú range to largely halt intra-tribal assassinations as well as warfare with the Achuara. In recent years, men who have engaged in such traditional raids have often been seized and sent off to an uncertain future in prison in the Ecuadorian highlands. These actions by the modern state have essentially brought interpersonal security to most of the Jívaro, thereby fundamentally altering the nature of the reality upon which much of their socio-economic structure and ideology were built. There are probably few cultures in the history of the world that have been so rapidly and significantly disintegrated by the simple introduction of centralized "law and order."

This does not mean that Jívaro killing has been entirely eliminated. In one locality east of the Cutucú's where there is no army garrison and the Achuara are nearby, feuding and warring still intermittently break out. However, it seems only a matter of time until this, too, will come to an end. More typical of the present situation is that some Jívaro are learning to conceal the evidence of murder along the lines perfected long ago in "civilized" societies. Thus they have recently begun to make assassinations appear to be deaths from natural causes (e.g., drowning) and to dispose of evidence of violent death by burying corpses or sinking them, weighted with stones, in rivers. Nonetheless, in totality, it does seem that violence has indeed declined substantially among the Jívaro.

An additional new development occurred in the lives of the Jívaro east of the Cutucú range when, in the latter part of 1971, at least one foreign-owned oil corporation began helicopter-supported operations in search of petroleum resources in their land. The consequences of these operations for the eastern portion of the tribe remain to be seen, but it appears that the native inhabitants of the land have no discernible voice regarding its exploitation.

While the traditional culture and society of the Jívaro are on the wane, their existence as a population certainly is not. Modern medical treatment and drugs provided primarily by missionaries have significantly contributed to a decline in mortality rates, especially among infants, and the estimated 7,830 *untsuri šuarä* of 1956–57 have now grown to a population for which estimates in 1969 ranged in the neighborhood of 15,000 persons. It is clear that the Jívaro have "turned the corner" demographically, and from what is known of North American Indian populations under similar circumstances, the prognosis would seem to be for a sustained continued growth.

Economic factors are also playing an important role in the rapidly changing life of these people. The Jívaro, as has been indicated earlier in this book, have long been anxious to acquire the technology and dress of Western civilization. Now that air transportation is available to most of the tribe, the only limit on Jívaro aspirations to acquire manufactured goods is their ability to acquire cash. Their model for such success is the cattle-raising Ecuadorian colonists west of the Cordillera de Cutucú, who have now converted most of the bottomlands of the Río Upano Valley into pasture with the aid of Jívaro labor. Air transport has made it profitable to ship beef to the highlands from there, and three local competing airlines are involved in the lucrative trade. Some Jívaro, with the strong encouragement of both Catholic and Protestant missionaries, are now clearing pasture land also for themselves to raise cattle and are starting to achieve success in acquiring substantial cash in exchange for beef.

While essentially pleased with their changing standard of living, the Jívaro have an increasingly pervasive fear of the white colonists and soldiers. West of the Cutucú range, the influx of mestizo settlers from the highlands has created a scarcity of land for cattle raising, and they are now attempting to invade the lands reserved by the Catholic missions for Indian use. The Jívaro, in turn, wish to expand their own pasture land, and see the attempted inroads by whites into the forest lands as a threat to their own future economic welfare. In 1969 a confrontation occurred between approximately four hundred Jívaro and thirty colonists and police near Sucúa when the latter group attempted to enter mission-administered lands. Although both groups were armed, no fighting broke out, the whites choosing to withdraw. However, the competition for land is clearly going to become worse, and may lead to serious bloodshed.

As of this writing, the last bridge is being constructed in a motor-vehicle road which is otherwise completed and which will connect Cuenca in the highlands with Macas via Méndez. This improved means of access to the Río Upano Valley will undoubtedly mean increased immigration of colonists from the province of Azuay.

Many members of the tribe seem convinced that the eventual goal of the whites is to wipe them out in order to seize their land. Throughout my stay in 1969 rumors swept through the Indian neighborhoods, even reaching as far as the Achuara, that the white soldiers were about to initiate such a massacre. Indeed, once, while my family and I were staying in a very isolated Achuara neighborhood near the Peruvian border, a rumor arrived (which we subsequently determined was erroneous) that Ecuadorian troops had killed five Jívaro men at Sucúa. Simply upon the basis of this most slender (mis)information, the Jívaro who accompanied us, together with our Achuara hosts, started planning to march on Sucúa to strike back. Thus there is a climate of hostility and unrest which recalls the conditions of the Jívaro revolt of 1599 and the near uprising of 1941.

An important aspect of the current situation is the difference between the concepts of land utilization held by the Jívaro and the whites. The Jívaro, with a free land tradition, have a difficult time adjusting to the concept of land ownership. Besides this, the Jívaro do not have the tradition of solely subsisting on agriculture and livestock raising, but also depend significantly upon hunting, fishing, and some gathering. Thus, in localities of high visibility to the whites, especially the mission-administered lands in the Río Upano Valley, the Indian lands appear to be unexploited by white standards, although the Jívaro feel that, in fact, their lands are overexploited in terms of hunting. Thus, while the Jívaro

believe that they lack adequate land, the whites feel that the
Indians are not using all the territory at their disposal. This
basic cultural difference makes successful communication and
adjudication of disputes extremely difficult between the two
groups. The Catholic Church, specifically the Salesian order,
which has the responsibility for the missions in the Upano
Valley, has generally chosen to side with the Indians, with
the result that it has alienated a large portion of the white
colonist population. Allegedly to show their displeasure, some
of the whites are reported to be responsible for burning down
a Salesian mission building at Sucúa in 1969.

The chief vehicle of Salesian support for the Jívaro is the
Federation of Shuar Centers (*Federación Provincial de Cen-
tros Shuaros de Morona-Santiago*) founded in 1964 with the
guidance of Padre Juan Shukta, and governed by Catholicized
Jívaro.[1] The organization, aiming at representing the economic, political and cultural interests of the majority of
Jívaro throughout the tribe, is attempting to encourage them
to develop a secure economic base through cattle raising,
creating pasture, and securing legal rights to their land. The
Federation also tries to encourage ethnic pride through brief
daily radio broadcasts transmitted in Jívaro from its new head-
quarters building in Sucúa. To this end, the native term,
"Shuar" (*šuarä*), has been adopted in preference to the formerly locally prevalent "Jíbaro," the latter term being felt to
connote "savage."

A serious problem for the Jívaro is that almost their only
spokesmen in the Ecuadorian power structure are the missionaries, since there has not been a branch of the government concerned specifically with the protection of the rights
of the forest Indians. Such a governmental agency would not
necessarily right the injustices to the Indians (witness the
many historic failures of the U. S. Bureau of Indian Af-

fairs), but the absence of such a third force to represent effectively the economic interests of the Jívaro within the governmental structure places the Indians under serious obligations to the missionaries and often limits their independence of action.

Still, the Jívaro have clearly opted for adaptation to a Western life style and seem to have no brief for maintaining traditional features of their native life simply for tradition's sake alone. While they undoubtedly will wish to preserve and even revive certain aspects of their old culture within the context of a desire for an ethnic identity, at this moment in time they seem to be basically focused upon acquiring what they discern as the most positive features of the whites' life. Whether their eventual fate will parallel that of their North American counterparts, who went through similar attempts at adaptation in the eighteenth and nineteenth centuries, or whether the twentieth century will be kinder, is a question that remains to be answered.

In any case, the culture of the Jívaro as described in this book now largely belongs to history. Personally, I view it as a loss, emotionally and scientifically, and only hope that these meager efforts will help preserve a record of what was once a magnificently distinctive life style.

BIBLIOGRAPHY

Anonymous
  1952   *Mons. Domingo Comin.* Cuenca: Talleres Gráficos Sales-
         ianos.
Barrueco, Domingo
  n.d.   *Historia de Macas.* Quito: Salesianos, Centro Misional de
         Investigaciones Científicas.
Bollaert, William
  1863   "On the Idol Human Head of the Jívaro Indians of Ec-
         uador, with a Translation of the Spanish Document Accom-
         panying It, the History of the Jívaro and their Conspiracy
         against the Spaniards in 1599." *Transactions of the Ethno-
         logical Society of London,* n.s., 2:112–18.
Castaneda, Carlos
  1968   *The Teachings of Don Juan: A Yaqui Way of Knowledge.*
         Berkeley and Los Angeles: University of California Press.
Cieza de León, Pedro de
  1943   *Del Señorío de los Incas* (Segunda Parte de la *Crónica del
         Perú*) [Reproduction of the text published by Marcos
         Jiménez de la Espada]. Buenos Aires: Ediciónes Argentinas
         "Solar."
Collier, Donald, and John V. Murra
  1943   *Survey and Excavations in Southern Ecuador.* Field Mu-
         seum of Natural History, Anthropological Series, Vol.
         35. Chicago.
Compte, Francisco Maria
  1885   *Varones Illustres de la Orden Seráfica en el Ecuador, desde
         la Fundación de Quito hasta nuestros Días,* Tomo 2. 2d
         edition. Quito: Imprenta del Clero.
Danielsson, Bengt
  1949   "Some Attraction and Repulsion Patterns among Jibaro
         Indians: A Study in Sociometric Anthropology." *Soci-
         ometry* 12:83–105.

Der Marderosian, A. H., H. V. Pinkley, and M. F. Dobbins IV.
1968 "Native Use and Occurrence of N,N-dimethyltryptamine in the Leaves of *Banisteriopsis rusbyana.*" *American Journal of Pharmacy* 140:137–47.

Dirección General de Estadística y Censos
1954 *Población por Idiomas y Dialectos. Primer Censo de Población del Ecuador:* 1950. Vol. 4, Tomo 1. Quito.

Drown, Frank and Marie
1961 *Mission to the Head-Hunters.* New York: Harper.

Ferdon, Edwin N., Jr.
1950 *Studies in Ecuadorian Geography.* Monographs of the School of American Research and Museum of New Mexico, 15. Santa Fe, New Mexico.

González Suárez, Federico
1890 *Historia General de la República del Ecuador.* Tomo 1. Quito: Imprenta del Clero.

Greenberg, Joseph H.
1960 "The General Classification of Central and South American Languages." In *Selected Papers, Fifth International Congress of Anthropological and Ethnological Sciences,* pp. 791–94. Philadelphia.

Harner, Michael J.
1962 "Jívaro Souls." *American Anthropologist* 64:258–72.
1963 *Machetes, Shotguns, and Society: An Inquiry into the Social Impact of Technological Change among the Jívaro Indians.* Unpublished Ph.D. dissertation, University of California, Berkeley.
1968a "The Sound of Rushing Water." *Natural History* 77(6): 28–33; 60–61.
1968b "Technological and Social Change among the Eastern Jívaro." In *XXXVII Congreso Internacional de Americanistas, Actas y Memorias, República Argentina–1966,* Vol. 1, pp. 363–88. Buenos Aires.
In Press (1) "The Role of Hallucinogenic Plants in European Witchcraft." In *Hallucinogens and Shamanism* (Michael J. Harner, ed.). New York: Oxford University Press.
In Press (2) *Music of the Jívaro.* Ethnic Folkways Album FE 4386. New York: Folkways Record and Service Corporation.

Herod, Dave D.
1970 *Type Versus Style: a Question of Comparability.* Un-

published M.A. thesis, San Francisco State College, San Francisco, California.

Jiménez de la Espada, Marcos (ed.)
1897 *Relaciones Geográficas de Indias.* Tomo 4, *Perú.* Madrid: Ministerio de Fomento.
1965 *Relaciones Geográficas de Indias. —Perú.* Tomo 3 [y 4]. Edición y estudio preliminar por José Urbano Martínez Carreras. Biblioteca de Autores Españoles, Tomo 185. Madrid: Ediciones Atlas.

Karsten, Rafael
1935 *The Head-hunters of Western Amazonas. The Life and Culture of the Jibaro Indians of Eastern Ecuador and Peru.* Societas Scientiarum Fennica, Commentationes Humanarum Litterarum, Vol. 7, No. 1. Helsinki.
1954 *Some Critical Remarks on Ethnological Field-research in South America.* Societas Scientarum Fennica, Commentationes Humanarum Litterarum, Vol. 19, No. 5. Helsinki.

Lucero, Juan Lorenzo
1892 "Suma de Carta . . . por el P. Juan Lorenzo Lucero de la Compañia de Jesús, . . . en que Da Cuenta . . . de los Sucesos que Acaecieron en la Entrada que Hizo á la Nacion de los Xíbaros." *Boletín de la Sociedad Geográfica de Madrid.* 33:24–44. Madrid.

Mason, J. Alden
1950 "The Languages of South American Indians." In *Handbook of South American Indians* (Julian H. Steward, ed.), Vol. 6, pp. 157–317. Bureau of American Ethnology Bulletin 143, Smithsonian Institution. Washington, D.C.

Murdock, George P.
1949 *Social Structure.* New York: Macmillan.

Platt, Raye R.
1932 "Opportunities for Agricultural Colonization in the Eastern Border Valleys of the Andes." In *Pioneer Settlement: Cooperative Studies by Twenty-six Authors* (W. L. G. Joerg, ed.), pp. 80–107. American Geographical Society, Special Publication No. 14. New York.

Reiss, W.
1880 "Ein Besuch bei den Jívaros-Indianern." *Verhandlungen der Gesellschaft für Erdkunde zu Berlin* 7:325–37.

Sollmann, Torald
1957 *A Manual of Pharmacology and Its Applications to Thera-*

peutics and Toxicology. Eighth edition. Philadelphia and London: W. B. Saunders.

Steere, William C.
1950 "The Phytogeography of Ecuador." Appendix in *Studies in Ecuadorian Geography* (E. N. Ferdon, Jr., ed.). Monographs of the School of American Research and Museum of New Mexico, 15:83–86. Santa Fe, New Mexico.

Stirling, M. W.
1938 *Historical and Ethnographical Material on the Jivaro Indians.* Bureau of American Ethnology Bulletin 117, Smithsonian Institution. Washington, D.C.

Turner, Glen D.
1958 "Alternative Phonemicizing in Jivaro." *International Journal of American Linguistics* 24:87–94.

Up de Graff, F. W.
1923 *Head Hunters of the Amazon. Seven Years of Exploration and Adventure.* Garden City, New York: Garden City Publishing.

Vacas Galindo, Enrique
1895 *Nankijukima. Religión, Usos y Costumbres de los Salvajes del Oriente del Ecuador.* Ambato: Merino.

Velasco, Juan de
1842 *Historia del Reino de Quito en la América Meridional. Año de 1789. Tomo 3 y pte. 3. La Historia Moderna.* Quito: Imprenta del Gobierno por J. Campusano.
n.d. *Historia Moderna del Reyno de Quito y Crónica de la Provincia de la Compañia de Jesús del mismo Reyno. Tomo 1. Años 1550 a 1685.* Publicación dirigida por Raúl Reyes y Reyes. Biblioteca Amazonas, Vol. 9. Quito.

Villavicencio, Manuel
1858 *Geografía de la República del Ecuador.* New York: Robert Craighead.

Wallis, Ethel E.
1965 *Tariri: My Story. From Jungle Killer to Christian Missionary.* London: Hodder and Stoughton.

NOTES

INTRODUCTION

1. Karsten, 1954, p. 7, pp. 10–31; Harner, 1962, pp. 268–70.
2. Harner, 1962. The excerpt from M. W. Stirling's letter is reproduced here with his kind permission.
3. The first general report on the research is embodied in Harner, 1963.

CHAPTER I

1. Jiménez de la Espada, 1965, Tomo 4, p. 175.
2. Mason, 1950, p. 222.
3. Greenberg, 1960, p. 794.
4. Determinations by the Yale University Geochronological Laboratories, whose assistance is gratefully acknowledged. Descriptions of the excavated pottery may be found in Herod, 1970.
5. Collier and Murra, 1943, pp. 61–62.
6. Jívaro is the name applied by Spanish speakers.
7. The "Mayna" Jivaroans have been reported in the Río Tigre region by workers of the Summer Institute of Linguistics. Little is known about them, and it is not clear if their dialect is more closely related to Jívaro or Achuara, and whether they form a distinct group.
8. Personal communication from David Beasley, Summer Institute of Linguistics, January 1961.
9. Personal communication from Mildred Larson, Summer Institute of Linguistics, January 1961.
10. This estimate is derived from a house count of Ecuadorian Jivaroans made from the air by personnel of the Summer Institute of Linguistics in 1956–57. To arrive at these population figures, the number of houses sighted was multiplied by an estimate of nine persons per dwelling. The aerial survey data were supplied by Glen Turner of the SIL (personal communication). Not included in this total are some 100 additional Jívaro emigrants residing in western Ecuador near the communities of Bucay and Santo Domingo de los Colorados.
11. The reader is reminded that the "ethnographic present" employed here refers to the period 1956–57. By 1969, only a few areas west of the Cutucú Mountains remained completely unpenetrated by white colonists.
12. The Huambisa appear to be very closely related to the *untsuri šuarä* in terms of dialect and details of culture. However, they

dwell south of the present Ecuadorian border, which prevented the author from visiting them and making a field comparison.

The Achuara, whom the author did visit, are frequently confused with the Jívaro in the literature and also are commonly included in the latter term by Ecuadorians who are not familiar with the distinctions between the two tribes or dialect groups. Salient cultural features that distinguish the Achuara from the Jívaro include the following: permanent matrilocality; weaving is done by the women; the women wear a topless skirt rather than a dress over one shoulder; the men's kilt is predominantly white rather than reddish-brown; two doors are commonly located in the women's end of the house; a stockade may be built outside the house in times of heightened hostilities; at other times houses often have no walls at all. The permanent matrilocality results in household populations considerably in excess of those normally found among the Jívaro, which has contributed to contradictions in the literature by explorers and others who were unaware, in fact, that they were among the Achuara.

13. Cieza de León, 1943, pp. 295–96; González Suárez, 1890, p. 54. Many of the sources cited by Stirling, 1938, in his compilation of historical materials, are not utilized here because they actually refer to Jivaroan groups other than the Jívaro proper (*untsuri šuarä*).

14. Jiménez de la Espada, 1965, Tomo 4, pp. 174–77.

15. It was probably at about this time that the Jívaro initially obtained chickens and pigs. The presence of pigs among the Jívaro is first definitely reported in 1683 by Lucero, 1892, p. 37. However, records are so fragmentary that it seems safe to assume that this report could have followed the actual inroduction by a century or longer.

16. Velasco, 1842, p. 151; Lucero, 1892, p. 33. The present writer is inclined to place Sevilla del Oro on the middle Río Upano (the Sucúa-Huambi area), because significant placer gold deposits do not occur on the upper portion of the river and because early reports of its latitude seem more consistent with such a location.

17. Jiménez de la Espada, 1897, p. 45. Translated by the author.

18. Velasco, 1842, p. 153; and n.d., p. 97.

19. Translated by the author from Velasco, 1842, pp. 153–57.

20. Lucero, 1892, p. 34.

21. Accounts of some of these ill-fated attempts may be found in Velasco, n.d., pp. 105–7; 203; 209–10; 286–288; and in Velasco, 1842, pp. 158–60.

22. Jiménez de la Espada, 1897, pp. 43–44.

23. Macabeo oral histories. Cf. also Barrueco, n.d.

24. Oral history provided by elderly Macabeos and Jívaro; Compte, 1885, p. 56; Vacas Galindo, 1895, p. 49; Villavicencio, 1858, pp. 366, 420–21.

25. From oral histories given by elderly Jívaro.

26. E.g., Bollaert, 1863.

27. Anonymous, 1952, p. 30. During the 1870's, the population of Macas was estimated to be 300 (Reiss, 1880, p. 329).

28. Vacas Galindo, 1895, pp. 49–50; Anonymous, 1952, p. 38.
29. Karsten, 1935, p. 8.
30. Anonymous, 1952, pp. 32–33; 38.
31. Platt, 1932, pp. 93–94.
32. Most of the following historical information is derived from oral accounts of older Ecuadorian colonists and Jívaro.
33. See Stirling, 1938, Plates 11–17.
34. Dirección General de Estadística y Censos, 1954, pp. 138; 141. These figures include the population of Macas. The Summer Institute of Linguistics aerial survey counted 256 Jívaro houses in the same region in 1956.
35. Drown, 1961, pp. 22, 31, 58–9, 140–44.
36. Macabeo and Jívaro oral histories.

CHAPTER II

1. Although rainfall is fairly heavy, it is well distributed throughout the year, and the distinct seasonal differences found in much of tropical forest South America are not as evident here. Short term records are available for rainfall and temperature at the Ecuadorian settlements of Macas, Méndez, and Gualaquiza, all in the higher western portion of the region. These reports of annual rainfall range from 1,992 mm. at Gualaquiza to 2,599 mm. at Méndez, with the minimum for a single month at any station being 95 mm. Recorded average temperatures from these same stations range from 21.4 to 25.2 degrees Centigrade (Ferdon, 1950, pp. 73–74).
2. Cf. Steere, 1950, p. 85.
3. In an earlier paper (Harner, 1962, p. 269) I questioned whether the Jívaro had any gods or goddesses, but additional field study and analysis have led me to be less certain of the classificatory status of Nuŋuí and, in fact, of the definition of "gods" and "goddesses" in general.
4. Demons lack blood.

CHAPTER III

1. Based upon a Summer Institute of Linguistics aerial survey in 1956–57 (Glen Turner, personal communication). The Jívaro population near the Macuma and Yaupi missions, comprising some eighty houses, is specifically excluded in the total here.
   The Summer Institute of Linguistics personnel were employing an intentionally conservative estimate of five persons per dwelling, which was used for earlier population estimates by the author (Harner, 1962, p. 259; 1963, p. 9; 1968b, p. 363). Additional research has led the author to revise the estimate of average household population upward to nine, and this is the figure employed in the present study. It seems impossible, however, to reconcile my results with those

reported by Danielsson (1949, p. 88) whose Jívaro families, and apparently households, are stated to range from 15 to 46 persons, with an average of approximately 30. Such figures may often occur among the Achuara, who practice permanent matrilocal residence, but Danielsson's study does not deal with that tribe. Two of Danielsson's neighborhoods, Patuca and Yurupaza, were encompassed by the Ecuadorian census of 1950 (Dirección General de Estadística y Censos, 1954, pp. 138; 141) of Jívaro in the Río Upano Valley and included in the aerial count of Jívaro houses by the Summer Institute of Linguistics in 1956–57. A comparison of the SIL Jívaro house count with the census figures for the Jívaro population in the Río Upano Valley, in which both the Patuca and Yurupaza neighborhoods are located, yields an average population of 9.2 persons per dwelling. On these grounds, as well as first-hand observations, it is difficult to accept Danielsson's "family" figures as representative household populations except under unusual circumstances. The few years separating these reports do not seem to be enough to account for this discrepancy and, in fact, informants' enumeration of the composition of earlier "large" households only rarely yielded figures beyond the range of 15 to 20 inhabitants.

2. Murdock, 1949, p. 60.

3. In the Jívaro language *kakaram* and *kakarma* are the same word, their last vowel and consonant being interchangeable, and the precise meaning is clarified by the morphological context. Since the word is being used here out of its linguistic context, *kakarma* is restricted to the designation of "power," and *kakaram* to the designation of "powerful one" in accordance with the observed tendency of use and in order to avoid confusion.

4. Elderly informants agree that the basic concept and practice of *amigri* trading partners in Jívaro culture antedates ca. 1910, although its intensification and elaboration are recent developments. The investigator failed to find any evidence of a historical connection between the Jívaro *amigü* concept and the Latin American *compadrazgo*. The frontier Jívaro and the Ecuadorians of Macas (the Macabeos) do reciprocally use the term *kumpa* (*compadre*) to address one another, but this is a general term used between any Macabeo and any Jívaro without the implication of personal obligation.

CHAPTER IV

1. *Arutam* may also be pronounced *arutma*, since the final vowel and consonant are interchangeable, as is the case with many Jívaro words. See Turner (1958) for a discussion of this and some other linguistic aspects of Jívaro.

2. Sollmann, 1957, pp. 381, 394.

3. Castaneda, 1968; and Harner, in press, (1).

4. One exception is the fireball *arutam*, which only vanishes silently when touched.

5. Persons who have seen *arutam* can be surprisingly well singled out by this trait alone. One of the recognized reasons a father helps his son acquire an *arutam* soul is so that a public awareness of his son's supernatural power to avenge will provide protection for the father in case the latter loses his own *arutam* soul(s).

6. There is also a rare super-*arutam*, *amuaŋ*, whose soul is not so easily satisfied and does not leave the body of its possessor when such declarations are made.

7. The *arutam* soul resident in the body of a person is *not* his *own* soul in any permanent sense, but only the soul of some ancestral Jívaro dwelling there temporarily.

8. Visitors to the Jívaro are usually impressed by the near shouting which typifies conversations between men of different households and neighborhoods. The functional basis for this custom can be seen in the desire of the individual to advertise his *arutam* power by being forceful in speech and gestures.

9. *Muisak* may alternatively be pronounced *muiska*.

10. When a man does not cut off the head of a person he has murdered (i.e., when the victim belongs to his own tribe), he turns the corpse face down on the ground so that the victim's *muisak* is delayed in emerging through the mouth. Thus the murderer hopes to reach home before the avenging soul can catch him.

11. A rather astonishing amount of misinformation has been published regarding the beliefs surrounding the *tsantsa*. I wish to re-emphasize that any contradictions between the information presented here and previous accounts indicates rejection of that material.

12. Possibly this is due to the fact that the old clearings provide feeding grounds for these animals.

13. Cf. Der Marderosian et al., 1968.

14. The mythological first shaman.

15. This is a halo of *tsentsak*, analogous to a feather "crown" sometimes worn by *kakaram*, which is seen as floating over the shaman's head (see Plate 24).

16. The breezes are caused by his *tsentsak* flying around.

17. Particularly on his shoulders.

18. The most powerful shamans (typically of the Canelos tribe) known to the Jívaro (see pp. 119–20).

CHAPTER V

1. Danielsson (1949, p. 92) mentions a dispute over river fishing rights in the Río Yurupaza neighborhood west of the Río Upano, but this is an area in which natural resource scarcity had already developed significantly as a consequence of immigration by white colonists from the province of Azuay.

2. The author has never participated in a war expedition, although he was invited to join one emanating from the Río Chiguasa region against the Achuara in 1957. The description which follows, therefore, is based entirely on informants' accounts.

3. The chant is recorded in Harner, in press (2).

4. The Jívaro, their Jivaroan neighbors, and the Candoshi are the only people within the past few centuries known to make the *tsantsa*. In addition, the Jívaro claim that the Achuara and the Huambisa learned the art from them in fairly recent times and formerly did not cut off heads in war. The Candoshi, in turn, state that they learned the practice fairly recently from the Achuara and Huambisa (Wallis, 1965, pp. 37–40). During the earlier decades of the present century, the craft was practiced by unscrupulous entrepreneurs using the heads of unclaimed dead in Guayaquil and Panama, which they passed off as Jívaro to tourists (see Karsten, 1935, pp. 81–82; Stirling, 1938, pp. 76–78; and Up de Graff, 1923, footnote, p. 283). Sometimes they went so far as to shrink the skins of entire bodies, a practice which, when I described it to Jívaro informants, was greeted with incredulity. The sale of shrunken heads is illegal in Ecuador and only imitations (although sometimes the sellers pretend they are not), made from monkey heads or the skins of other animals, now seem to be marketed.

5. Name of the victim. The victim's name is usually learned from captured women or from persons who have interacted with the Achuara in trade.

CHAPTER VI

1. The appearance of this comet is well remembered, and in fact informants recalled that in one neighborhood some Jívaro attempted to reach it by building a wooden tower!

2. Vacas Galindo, 1895, p. 49; Compte, 1885, p. 56; and oral histories recorded by the author.

3. *Head Hunters of the Amazon* by F. W. Up de Graff, 1923 (Dodd, Mead and Company).

4. The introduction of a few steel tools to the frontier Jívaro in the vicinity of Macas in the mid-nineteenth century may have increased garden size and production at that time, judging from oral traditions. However, oral information on events so far in the past is not included as evidence in this account of cultural change. A previous version of this material, with comparative data, appeared in Harner, 1968b.

EPILOGUE

1. I am indebted to Padre Shukta and Peter Hart for their assistance in obtaining some of the information contained in this section.

INDEX

MICHAEL J. HARNER is Associate Professor of Anthropology on the Graduate Faculty of the New School for Social Research in New York. He has taught at various universities including Columbia, Yale, the University of California at Berkeley (where he received his Ph.D.), and has served as Assistant Director of the Robert H. Lowie Museum of Anthropology at Berkeley.

Born in Washington, D.C., in 1929, Dr. Harner spent the earliest years of his childhood in South America. He returned there to do fieldwork among the Jívaro Indians of Ecuador in 1956 and 1957 and the Conibo Indians of Peru in 1960 and 1961. In 1964 and 1969 he pursued additional field studies of the Jívaro and made an expedition to the Jivaroan Achuara tribe.